CONNECTED MATHEMATICS

Moving Straight Ahead

Linear Relationships

Glenda Lappan, Elizabeth Difanis Phillips,
James T. Fey, Susan N. Friel

PEARSON

Boston, Massachusetts • Chandler, Arizona • Glenview, Illinois • Hoboken, New Jersey

Connected Mathematics® was developed at Michigan State University with financial support from the Michigan State University Office of the Provost, Computing and Technology, and the College of Natural Science.

This material is based upon work supported by the National Science Foundation under Grant No. MDR 9150217 and Grant No. ESI 9986372. Opinions expressed are those of the authors and not necessarily those of the Foundation.

As with prior editions of this work, the authors and administration of Michigan State University preserve a tradition of devoting royalties from this publication to support activities sponsored by the MSU Mathematics Education Enrichment Fund.

Acknowledgments appear on page 133, which constitutes an extension of this copyright page.

13-digit ISBN 978-0-13-327639-8
10-digit ISBN 0-13-327639-2
5 6 7 8 9 10 V011 17 16 15

A Team of Experts

Glenda Lappan is a University Distinguished Professor in the Program in Mathematics Education (PRIME) and the Department of Mathematics at Michigan State University. Her research and development interests are in the connected areas of students' learning of mathematics and mathematics teachers' professional growth and change related to the development and enactment of K–12 curriculum materials.

Elizabeth Difanis Phillips is a Senior Academic Specialist in the Program in Mathematics Education (PRIME) and the Department of Mathematics at Michigan State University. She is interested in teaching and learning mathematics for both teachers and students. These interests have led to curriculum and professional development projects at the middle school and high school levels, as well as projects related to the teaching and learning of algebra across the grades.

James T. Fey is a Professor Emeritus at the University of Maryland. His consistent professional interest has been development and research focused on curriculum materials that engage middle and high school students in problem-based collaborative investigations of mathematical ideas and their applications.

Susan N. Friel is a Professor of Mathematics Education in the School of Education at the University of North Carolina at Chapel Hill. Her research interests focus on statistics education for middle-grade students and, more broadly, on teachers' professional development and growth in teaching mathematics K–8.

With... Yvonne Grant and Jacqueline Stewart

Yvonne Grant teaches mathematics at Portland Middle School in Portland, Michigan. Jacqueline Stewart is a recently retired high school teacher of mathematics at Okemos High School in Okemos, Michigan. Both Yvonne and Jacqueline have worked on a variety of activities related to the development, implementation, and professional development of the CMP curriculum since its beginning in 1991.

Development Team

CMP3 Authors

Glenda Lappan, University Distinguished Professor, Michigan State University

Elizabeth Difanis Phillips, Senior Academic Specialist, Michigan State University

James T. Fey, Professor Emeritus, University of Maryland

Susan N. Friel, Professor, University of North Carolina – Chapel Hill

With...

Yvonne Grant, Portland Middle School, Michigan

Jacqueline Stewart, Mathematics Consultant, Mason, Michigan

In Memory of... William M. Fitzgerald, Professor (Deceased), Michigan State University, who made substantial contributions to conceptualizing and creating CMP1.

Administrative Assistant

Michigan State University
Judith Martus Miller

Support Staff

Michigan State University
Undergraduate Assistants:
Bradley Robert Corlett, Carly Fleming, Erin Lucian, Scooter Nowak

Development Assistants

Michigan State University
Graduate Research Assistants:
Richard "Abe" Edwards, Nic Gilbertson, Funda Gonulates, Aladar Horvath, Eun Mi Kim, Kevin Lawrence, Jennifer Nimtz, Joanne Philhower, Sasha Wang

Assessment Team

Maine
Falmouth Public Schools
Falmouth Middle School: Shawn Towle

Michigan
Ann Arbor Public Schools
Tappan Middle School
Anne Marie Nicoll-Turner

Portland Public Schools
Portland Middle School
Holly DeRosia, Yvonne Grant

Traverse City Area Public Schools
Traverse City East Middle School
Jane Porath, Mary Beth Schmitt

Traverse City West Middle School
Jennifer Rundio, Karrie Tufts

Ohio
Clark-Shawnee Local Schools
Rockway Middle School: Jim Mamer

Content Consultants

Michigan State University
Peter Lappan, Professor Emeritus, Department of Mathematics

Normandale Community College
Christopher Danielson, Instructor, Department of Mathematics & Statistics

University of North Carolina – Wilmington
Dargan Frierson, Jr., Professor, Department of Mathematics & Statistics

Student Activities
Michigan State University
Brin Keller, Associate Professor, Department of Mathematics

Consultants

Indiana
Purdue University
Mary Bouck, Mathematics Consultant

Michigan
Oakland Schools
Valerie Mills, Mathematics Education Supervisor
Mathematics Education Consultants:
Geraldine Devine, Dana Gosen

Ellen Bacon, Independent Mathematics Consultant

New York
University of Rochester
Jeffrey Choppin, Associate Professor

Ohio
University of Toledo
Debra Johanning, Associate Professor

Pennsylvania
University of Pittsburgh
Margaret Smith, Professor

Texas
University of Texas at Austin
Emma Trevino, Supervisor of Mathematics Programs, The Dana Center

Mathematics for All Consulting
Carmen Whitman, Mathematics Consultant

Reviewers

Michigan
Ionia Public Schools
Kathy Dole, Director of Curriculum and Instruction

Grand Valley State University
Lisa Kasmer, Assistant Professor

Portland Public Schools
Teri Keusch, Classroom Teacher

Minnesota
Hopkins School District 270
Michele Luke, Mathematics Coordinator

Field Test Sites for CMP3

Michigan
Ann Arbor Public Schools
Tappan Middle School
Anne Marie Nicoll-Turner*

Portland Public Schools
Portland Middle School: Mark Braun,
Angela Buckland, Holly DeRosia,
Holly Feldpausch, Angela Foote,
Yvonne Grant*, Kristin Roberts,
Angie Stump, Tammi Wardwell

Traverse City Area Public Schools
Traverse City East Middle School
Ivanka Baic Berkshire, Brenda Dunscombe,
Tracie Herzberg, Deb Larimer, Jan Palkowski,
Rebecca Perreault, Jane Porath*,
Robert Sagan, Mary Beth Schmitt*

Traverse City West Middle School
Pamela Alfieri, Jennifer Rundio,
Maria Taplin, Karrie Tufts*

Maine
Falmouth Public Schools
Falmouth Middle School: Sally Bennett,
Chris Driscoll, Sara Jones, Shawn Towle*

Minnesota
Minneapolis Public Schools
Jefferson Community School
Leif Carlson*,
Katrina Hayek Munsisoumang*

Ohio
Clark-Shawnee Local Schools
Reid School: Joanne Gilley
Rockway Middle School: Jim Mamer*
Possum School: Tami Thomas

*Indicates a Field Test Site Coordinator

Moving Straight Ahead

Linear Relationships

Looking Ahead

Grace's walking rate is 1.5 meters per second. Her house is 90 meters from the fountain. **How** many seconds will it take her to reach the fountain? It takes Allie 45 seconds to walk from Grace's house to the fountain. **What** is Allie's walking rate?

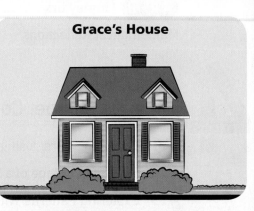

Grace's House

Forensic scientists can estimate a person's height by measuring the lengths of certain bones. **What** is the approximate height of a male whose tibia is 50.1 centimeters long?

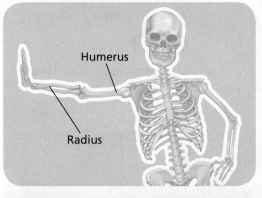

Humerus

Radius

Robert is installing a patio in his backyard. At 2:00 P.M., he has 120 stones laid in the ground. At 3:30 P.M., he has 180 stones in the ground. **When** will he be done?

All around you, things occur in patterns. Once you observe a pattern, you can use it to predict information beyond and between the data observed. The ability to use patterns to make predictions makes it possible for a baseball player to run to the right position to catch a fly ball or for a pilot to estimate the flying time for a trip.

In *Variables and Patterns*, you investigated relationships between variables. The relationships were displayed as verbal descriptions, tables, graphs, and equations. Some of the graphs, such as the graph of distance and time for a van traveling at a steady rate, were straight lines. Relationships with graphs that are straight lines are called *linear relationships*.

In this Unit, you will study linear relationships. You will learn about the characteristics of a linear relationship. You will determine whether a relationship is linear by looking at its equation or at a table of values. You will also learn how to solve linear equations. You will use what you learn about linear relationships to answer questions like those on the facing page.

Mathematical Highlights

Linear Relationships

In *Moving Straight Ahead*, you will explore properties of linear relationships and linear equations.

You will learn how to:

- Recognize problem situations that involve linear relationships

- Construct tables, graphs, and symbolic equations that represent linear relationships

- Translate information about linear relations given in a verbal description, a table, a graph, or an equation to one of the other forms

- Connect equations that represent linear relationships to the patterns in tables and graphs of those equations

- Identify the rate of change, slope, and *y*-intercept from the graph of a linear relationship

- Solve linear equations

- Write and interpret equivalent expressions as well as determine whether two or more expressions are equivalent

- Solve problems and make decisions about linear relationships using information given in tables, graphs, and equations

- Solve problems that can be modeled with inequalities and graph the solution set

When you encounter a new problem, it is a good idea to ask yourself questions. In this Unit, you might ask questions such as:

What are the variables in the problem?

Do the variables in the problem have a linear relationship to each other?

What patterns in the problem suggest that the relationship is linear?

How can the linear relationship in a situation be represented with a verbal description, a table, a graph, or an equation?

How do changes in one variable affect changes in a related variable?

How are these changes captured in a table, a graph, or an equation?

How can tables, graphs, and equations of linear relationships be used to answer questions?

Mathematical Practices and Habits of Mind

In the *Connected Mathematics* curriculum you will develop an understanding of important mathematical ideas by solving problems and reflecting on the mathematics involved. Every day, you will use "habits of mind" to make sense of problems and apply what you learn to new situations. Some of these habits are described by the *Common Core State Standards for Mathematical Practices* (MP).

MP1 Make sense of problems and persevere in solving them.

When using mathematics to solve a problem, it helps to think carefully about

- data and other facts you are given and what additional information you need to solve the problem;
- strategies you have used to solve similar problems and whether you could solve a related simpler problem first;
- how you could express the problem with equations, diagrams, or graphs;
- whether your answer makes sense.

MP2 Reason abstractly and quantitatively.

When you are asked to solve a problem, it often helps to

- focus first on the key mathematical ideas;
- check that your answer makes sense in the problem setting;
- use what you know about the problem setting to guide your mathematical reasoning.

MP3 Construct viable arguments and critique the reasoning of others.

When you are asked to explain why a conjecture is correct, you can

- show some examples that fit the claim and explain why they fit;
- show how a new result follows logically from known facts and principles.

When you believe a mathematical claim is incorrect, you can

- show one or more counterexamples—cases that don't fit the claim;
- find steps in the argument that do not follow logically from prior claims.

MP4 Model with mathematics.

When you are asked to solve problems, it often helps to

- think carefully about the numbers or geometric shapes that are the most important factors in the problem, then ask yourself how those factors are related to each other;
- express data and relationships in the problem with tables, graphs, diagrams, or equations, and check your result to see if it makes sense.

MP5 Use appropriate tools strategically.

When working on mathematical questions, you should always

- decide which tools are most helpful for solving the problem and why;
- try a different tool when you get stuck.

MP6 Attend to precision.

In every mathematical exploration or problem-solving task, it is important to

- think carefully about the required accuracy of results; is a number estimate or geometric sketch good enough, or is a precise value or drawing needed?
- report your discoveries with clear and correct mathematical language that can be understood by those to whom you are speaking or writing.

MP7 Look for and make use of structure.

In mathematical explorations and problem solving, it is often helpful to

- look for patterns that show how data points, numbers, or geometric shapes are related to each other;
- use patterns to make predictions.

MP8 Look for and express regularity in repeated reasoning.

When results of a repeated calculation show a pattern, it helps to

- express that pattern as a general rule that can be used in similar cases;
- look for shortcuts that will make the calculation simpler in other cases.

You will use all of the Mathematical Practices in this Unit. Sometimes, when you look at a Problem, it is obvious which practice is most helpful. At other times, you will decide on a practice to use during class explorations and discussions. After completing each Problem, ask yourself:

> **?** • What mathematics have I learned by solving this Problem?
>
> • What Mathematical Practices were helpful in learning this mathematics?

Walking Rates

In *Variables and Patterns*, you read about a bicycle touring business. You used contextual situations, tables, graphs, and equations to represent patterns relating variables such as cost, income, and profit. You looked at some linear relationships, like the relationship between cost and number of rental bikes represented in this graph:

A relationship between two variables for which all points lie on a straight line is called a **linear relationship.** From the graph, you see that the relationship between the number of bikes rented and the total rental cost is a linear relationship. In this Investigation, consider these questions:

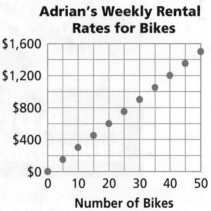

Adrian's Weekly Rental Rates for Bikes

- How can you determine whether a relationship is linear by examining a table of data or an equation?

- How do changes in one variable affect changes in a related variable? How are these changes captured in a table, a graph, or an equation?

....

Common Core State Standards

7.RP.A.2b Identify the constant of proportionality (unit rate) in tables, graphs, equations, diagrams, and verbal descriptions of proportional relationships.

7.RP.A.2c Represent proportional relationships by equations.

7.EE.B.4 Use variables to represent quantities in a real-world or mathematical problem, and construct simple equations and inequalities to solve problems by reasoning about the quantities.

Also 7.RP.A.2, 7.RP.A.2a, 7.EE.B.4a

1.1 Walking Marathons
Finding and Using Rates

Ms. Chang's class decides to participate in a walkathon. Each participant must find sponsors to pledge a certain amount of money for each kilometer the participant walks. Leanne suggests that they determine their walking rates in meters per second so they can make predictions.

- Do you know what your walking rate is?

- How can you determine your walking rate?

Problem 1.1

One way to define your walking rate is the distance you walk for every second of walking time.

To determine your walking rate:

- Line up ten meter sticks, end to end (or mark off 10 meters), in the hall of your school.

- Have a partner time your walk.

- Start at one end and walk the length of the ten meter sticks using your normal walking pace.

A What is your walking rate in meters per second?

B Assume you continue to walk at this constant rate.

   1. How long would it take you to walk 500 meters?

   2. How far could you walk in 30 seconds? In 10 minutes? In 1 hour?

   3. Describe in words the distance in meters you could walk in a given number of seconds.

   4. Write an equation that represents the distance d in meters that you could walk in t seconds if you maintain this pace.

   5. Use the equation to predict the distance you would walk in 45 seconds.

 Homework starts on page 16.

1.2 Walking Rates and Linear Relationships

Tables, Graphs, and Equations

Think about the effect a walking rate has on the relationship between time walked and distance walked. This will provide some important clues about how to identify linear relationships from tables, graphs, and equations.

Problem 1.2

Here are the walking rates that Gilberto, Alana, and Leanne found in their experiment.

A 1. Make a table showing the distance walked by each student for the first ten seconds. How does the walking rate appear as a pattern in the table?

Name	Walking Rate
Alana	1 meter per second
Gilberto	2 meters per second
Leanne	2.5 meters per second

2. Graph the times and distances for the three students on the same coordinate axes. Use a different color for each student's data. How does the walking rate affect the graph?

3. Write an equation that gives the relationship between the time t and the distance d walked for each student. How is the walking rate represented in the equations?

4. How can you predict that the graph will be a straight line from the patterns in the table? In the equation? Explain.

5. Are any of these proportional relationships? If so, what is the constant of proportionality?

B For each student:

1. If time t increases by 1 second, by how much does the distance d change? How is this change represented in a table? In a graph?

2. If t increases by 5 seconds, by how much does d change? How is this change represented in a table? In a graph?

3. What is the walking rate per minute? The walking rate per hour?

Problem 1.2 *continued*

C Four other friends who are part of the walkathon made the following representations of their data. Could any of these relationships be linear relationships? Explain.

George's Walking Rate

Time (seconds)	Distance (meters)
0	0
1	2
2	9
3	11
4	20
5	25

Elizabeth's Walking Rate

Time (seconds)	Distance (meters)
0	0
2	3
4	6
6	9
8	12
10	15

Billie's Walking Rate
$D = 2.25t$

D represents distance
t represents time

Bob's Walking Rate
$$t = \frac{100}{r}$$

t represents time
r represents walking rate

A C E Homework starts on page 16.

1.3 Raising Money
Using Linear Relationships

In *Variables and Patterns*, you looked at situations that involved *dependent* and *independent* variables. In Problem 1.2, the distance walked depended on the time. This tells you that distance is the **dependent variable** and time is the **independent variable**. In this Problem, you will look at relationships between two other variables in a walkathon.

Each participant in the walkathon must find sponsors to pledge a certain amount of money for each kilometer the participant walks.

The students in Ms. Chang's class are trying to estimate how much money they might be able to raise. Several questions come up in their discussions:

- What variables can affect the amount of money that is collected?

- How can you use these variables to estimate the amount of money each student will collect?

- Will the amount of money collected be the same for each walker?

Each student found sponsors who are willing to pledge money according to the following descriptions.

- Leanne's sponsors will donate $10 regardless of how far she walks.

- Gilberto's sponsors will donate $2 per kilometer (km).

- Alana's sponsors will make a $5 donation plus 50¢ per kilometer.

The class refers to these as *pledge plans*.

Tables, graphs, and equations will help you predict how much money might be raised with each plan.

- What are the dependent and independent variables?

Walkathon!

Pledge Sheet

Walker: _Gilberto_

Kilometers Walked: _____

Sponsor's Name	Donation	Amount Pledged per Kilometer	Amount Paid
	$	$	
	$	$	$
	$	$	$
	$	$	$
	$	$	$
			$
		TOTAL $	

? Who will raise the most money after *d* kilometers?

Problem 1.3

A 1. Make a table for each student's pledge plan. Show the amount of money each of his or her sponsors would donate if he or she walked distances from 0 to 6 kilometers. What are the dependent and independent variables?

2. Graph the three pledge plans on the same coordinate axes. Use a different color for each plan.

Problem 1.3 *continued*

3. For each pledge plan, write an equation that represents the relationship between the distance walked and the amount of money donated. Explain what information each number and variable in the equations represents.

4. For each plan:

   a. What pattern of change between the two variables do you observe in the table?

   b. How does this pattern appear in the graph? In the equation?

   c. How can you determine if a relationship is linear from a table, a graph, or an equation?

   d. Does this relationship represent a proportional relationship?

B 1. Suppose each student walks 8 kilometers in the walkathon. How much money does each sponsor donate? Explain how you found your answer.

   2. Suppose each student raises $10 from a sponsor. How many kilometers does each student walk? Explain.

   3. On which graph does the point (12, 11) lie? What information does this point represent?

   4. In Alana's plan, how is the fixed $5 donation represented in

      a. the table?

      b. the graph?

      c. the equation?

C Gilberto decides to give a T-shirt to each of his sponsors. Each shirt costs him $4.75. He plans to pay for each shirt with some of the money he raises from each sponsor.

   1. Write an equation that represents the amount of money Gilberto raises from each sponsor after he has paid for the T-shirt. Explain what information each number and variable represents.

   2. Graph the equation for distances from 0 to 5 kilometers. Compare this graph to the graph of Gilberto's pledge plan in Question A, part (2).

   3. Is this relationship linear? Explain.

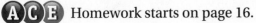 Homework starts on page 16.

1.4 Using the Walkathon Money
Recognizing Linear Relationships

In previous Problems, you noticed that, as the independent variable changes by a constant amount, there is a pattern of change in the dependent variable. You can use this pattern of change to identify other linear relationships.

Ms. Chang's class decides to use their money from the walkathon to provide books for the children's ward at the hospital. The class puts the money in the school safe and withdraws a fixed amount each week to buy new books. To keep track of the money, Isabella makes a table of the amount of money in the account at the end of each week.

Week	Amount of Money at the End of Each Week
0	$144
1	$132
2	$120
3	$108
4	$96
5	$84

- What do you think the graph of this data would look like?

- Does this table represent a linear relationship? How did you decide?

Problem 1.4

A 1. How much money is in the account at the start of the project? Explain.

2. How much money is withdrawn from the account each week?

3. Suppose the students continue withdrawing the same amount of money each week. Sketch a graph of this relationship.

4. Write an equation that represents the relationship. Explain what information each number and variable represents.

5. Is the relationship between the number of weeks and the amount of money left in the account linear? Explain.

Problem **1.4** *continued*

B Mr. Mamer's class also raised money from the walkathon. They use the money to buy games and puzzles for the children's ward. Keenan uses a graph to keep track of the amount of money in the account at the end of each week.

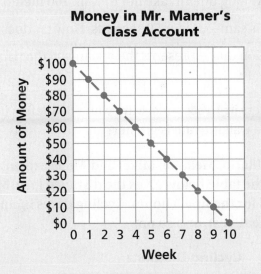

Money in Mr. Mamer's Class Account

1. What information does the graph represent about the money in Mr. Mamer's class account?

2. Make a table of data for the first 10 weeks. Explain why this table represents a linear relationship.

3. Write the equation that models the linear relationship. Explain what information each number and variable represents.

C 1. How can you determine whether a relationship is linear from a graph, a table, or an equation?

2. Compare the patterns of change for the linear relationships in this Problem to those in previous Problems in this Investigation.

ACE Homework starts on page 16.

Applications

1. Hoshi walks 10 meters in 3 seconds.

   a. What is her walking rate?

   b. At this rate, how long does it take her to walk 100 meters?

   c. She walks at this same rate for 50 seconds. How far does she walk?

   d. Write an equation that represents the distance d that Hoshi walks in t seconds.

2. Milo walks 40 meters in 15 seconds. Mira walks 30 meters in 10 seconds. Whose walking rate is greater?

For Exercises 3–5, Jose, Mario, Melanie, Mike, and Alicia are on a weeklong cycling trip. The table below gives the distance Jose, Mario, and Melanie each travel for the first 3 hours. Cycling times include only biking time, not time to eat, rest, and so on.

Cycling Distance

Cycling Time (hours)	Distance (miles)		
	Jose	Mario	Melanie
0	0	0	0
1	5	7	9
2	10	14	18
3	15	21	27

3. **a.** Assume that each person cycles at a constant rate. Find the rate at which each person travels during the first 3 hours. Explain.

   b. Find the distance each person travels in 7 hours.

   c. Graph the time and distance data for all three riders on the same coordinate axes.

   d. Use the graphs to find the distance each person travels in $6\frac{1}{2}$ hours.

   e. Use the graphs to find the time it takes each person to travel 70 miles.

f. How does the rate at which each person rides affect each graph?

g. For each rider, write an equation that can be used to calculate the distance traveled after a given number of hours.

h. Use your equations from part (g) to calculate the distance each person travels in $6\frac{1}{2}$ hours.

i. How does a person's cycling rate show up in his or her equation?

j. Are any of these proportional relationships? If so, what is the constant of proportionality?

4. Mike makes the following table of the distances he travels during the first day of the trip.

a. Suppose Mike continues riding at this rate. Write an equation for the distance Mike travels after t hours.

b. Sketch a graph of the equation. How did you choose the range of values for the time axis? For the distance axis?

c. How can you find the distances Mike travels in 7 hours and in $9\frac{1}{2}$ hours, using the table? Using the graph? Using the equation?

d. How can you find the numbers of hours it takes Mike to travel 100 miles and 237 miles, using the table? Using the graph? Using the equation?

Cycling Distance

Time (hours)	Distance (miles)
0	0
1	6.5
2	13
3	19.5
4	26
5	32.5
6	39

e. For parts (c) and (d), what are the advantages and disadvantages of using each model—a table, a graph, and an equation—to find the answers?

f. Compare the rate at which Mike rides with the rates at which Jose, Mario, and Melanie ride. Who rides the fastest? How can you determine this from the tables? From the graphs? From the equations?

5. The distance in miles Alicia travels in t hours is represented by the equation $d = 7.5t$.

a. At what rate does Alicia travel? Explain.

b. Suppose the graph of Alicia's distance and time is put on the same set of axes as Mike's, Jose's, Mario's, and Melanie's graphs. Where would it be located in relationship to each of the graphs? Describe the location without actually making the graph.

6. The graph below represents the walkathon pledge plans for three sponsors.

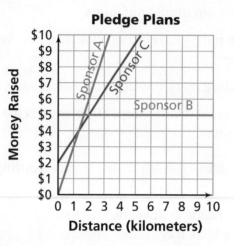

Pledge Plans

a. Describe each sponsor's pledge plan.

b. What is the number of dollars per kilometer each sponsor pledges?

c. What does the point where the line crosses the *y*-axis mean for each sponsor?

d. Write the coordinates of two points on each line. What information does each point represent for the sponsor's pledge plan?

e. Does each relationship represent a proportional relationship?

7. The students in Ms. Chang's class decide to order water bottles that advertise the walkathon. Hyun obtains two different quotes for the costs of the bottles.

a. For each company, write an equation Hyun could use to calculate the cost for any number of bottles.

b. On the same set of axes, graph both equations from part (a). Which variable is the independent variable? Which is the dependent variable?

c. From which company do you think the class should buy water bottles? What factors influenced your decision?

d. For what number of water bottles is the cost the same for both companies? Explain.

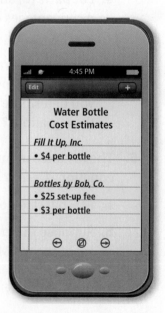

4:45 PM

Edit

Water Bottle Cost Estimates

Fill It Up, Inc.
• $4 per bottle

Bottles by Bob, Co.
• $25 set-up fee
• $3 per bottle

8. **Multiple Choice** The equation $C = 5n$ represents the cost C in dollars for n caps that advertise the walkathon. Which of the following ordered pairs could represent a number of caps and the cost for that number of caps, (n, C)?

   A. $(0, 5)$ **B.** $(3, 15)$ **C.** $(15, 60)$ **D.** $(5, 1)$

9. The equation $d = 3.5t + 50$ gives the distance d in meters that a cyclist is from his home after t seconds.

   a. Which of the following ordered pairs represents a point on the graph of this equation? Explain your answer.

   i. $(10, 85)$ **ii.** $(0, 0)$ **iii.** $(3, 60.5)$

   b. What information do the coordinates tell you about the cyclist?

10. Examine the pattern in each table.

Table 1			Table 2			Table 3			Table 4	
x	y		x	y		x	y		x	y
-2	3		-3	9		0	10		0	-3
-1	3		-2	4		3	19		2	-6
0	3		-1	1		5	25		4	-9
1	3		0	0		10	40		6	-12
2	3		1	1		12	46		8	-15

   a. Describe the similarities and differences in Tables 1–4.

   b. Explain how you can use each table to decide whether the data indicate a linear relationship between the two quantities.

   c. Sketch a graph of the data in each table.

   d. Write an equation that represents the relationship between the independent and dependent variables for each linear relationship. Explain what information the numbers and variables tell you about the relationship.

11. **a.** The temperature at the North Pole is 30°F and is expected to drop 5°F per hour for the next several hours. Write an equation that represents the relationship between temperature and time. Explain what information your numbers and variables represent.

   b. Is this a linear relationship? Explain your reasoning.

12. Jamal's parents give him money to spend at camp. Jamal spends the same amount of money on snacks each day. The table below shows the amount of money, in dollars, he has left at the end of each day.

Snack Money

Days	0	1	2	3	4	5	6
Money Left	$20	$18	$16	$14	$12	$10	$8

   a. How much money does Jamal have at the start of camp? Explain.

   b. How much money does he spend each day? Explain.

   c. Is the relationship between the number of days and the amount of money left in Jamal's wallet a linear relationship? Explain.

   d. Assume that Jamal's spending pattern continues. Check your answer to part (c) by sketching a graph of this relationship.

   e. Write an equation that represents the relationship. Explain what information the numbers and variables represent.

13. Write an equation for each graph.

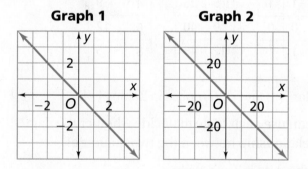

Graph 1   **Graph 2**

14. **a.** Describe a situation that involves a linear relationship between an independent variable and a dependent variable for which the rate of change is:

   i. positive.   **ii.** zero (no change).   **iii.** negative.

   b. Write an equation that models each situation in part (a).

Connections

15. Jelani is in a walking race at his school. In the first 20 seconds, he walks 60 meters. In the next 30 seconds, he walks 60 meters. In the next 10 seconds, he walks 35 meters. In the last 40 seconds, he walks 80 meters.

   a. Describe how Jelani's walking rate changes during the race.

   b. What would a graph of Jelani's walking race look like?

16. Insert parentheses in the expression on the left side of each equation to make each number sentence true.

   a. $2 + -3 \times 4 = -10$

   b. $4 + -3 \times -4 = -4$

   c. $-12 \div 2 + -4 = 6$

   d. $8 \div -2 + -2 = -6$

17. Which of the following number sentences are true? In each case, explain how you could answer without any calculation. Check your answers by doing the indicated calculations.

   a. $20 \times 410 = (20 \times 400) + (20 \times 10)$

   b. $20 \times 308 = (20 \times 340) - (20 \times 32)$

   c. $-20 \times -800 = (-20 \times -1{,}000) + (-20 \times 200)$

   d. $-20 + (300 \times 32) = (-20 + 300) \times (-20 + 32)$

18. Fill in the missing parts to make each number sentence true.

   a. $15 \times (6 + 4) = (15 \times \blacksquare) + (15 \times 4)$

   b. $2 \times (x + 6) = (2 \times \blacksquare) + (\blacksquare \times 6)$

   c. $(x \times 2) + (x \times 6) = \blacksquare \times (2 + 6)$

19. a. Draw a rectangle whose area can be represented by the expression $5 \times (12 + 6)$.

   b. Write another expression to represent the area of the rectangle in part (a).

20. Find the unit rate and use it to write an equation relating the two quantities.

   a. 150 dollars for 50 T-shirts

   b. 62 dollars to rent 14 video games

   c. 18 tablespoons of sugar in 3 glasses of Bolda Cola

21. The longest human-powered sporting event is the Tour de France cycling race. In a particular year, the average speed for the winner of this race was 23.66 miles per hour.

   a. In that same year, the race was 2,292 miles long. How long did it take the winner to complete the race?

   b. Suppose the winner had reduced his average cycling rate by 0.1 mile per hour. By how much would his time have changed?

22. a. In 1990, Nadezhda Ryashkina set the record for the 10,000 m race-walking event. She finished this race in 41 minutes 56.23 seconds. What was Ryashkina's average walking rate, in meters per second?

   b. In 2001, Olimpiada Ivanova set the record for the 20,000 m race-walking event. She finished the race in 86 minutes 52.3 seconds. What was Ivanova's average walking speed, in meters per second?

23. A recipe for orange juice calls for 2 cups of orange juice concentrate and 3 cups of water. The table below shows the amount of concentrate and water needed to make a given number of batches of juice.

Orange Juice Mixture Amounts

Batches of Juice (b)	Concentrate (c)	Water (w)	Juice (j)
1	2 cups	3 cups	5 cups
2	4 cups	6 cups	10 cups
3	6 cups	9 cups	15 cups
4	8 cups	12 cups	20 cups

The relationship between the number of batches of juice b and the number of cups of concentrate c is linear. The equation that represents this linear relationship is $c = 2b$. Are there other relationships in this table that are linear? Sketch graphs or write equations for any you find.

24. The table below shows the number of cups of orange juice, pineapple juice, and soda water needed for different quantities of punch.

Pineapple Punch Recipe

J (orange juice, cups)	P (pineapple juice, cups)	S (soda water, cups)
1	▪	▪
2	▪	▪
3	▪	▪
4	12	6
5	▪	▪
6	▪	▪
7	▪	▪
8	24	12

The relationship between cups of orange juice and cups of pineapple juice is linear. The relationship between cups of orange juice and cups of soda water is also linear.

a. Zahara makes the recipe using 6 cups of orange juice. How many cups of soda water does she use? Explain your reasoning.

b. Patrick makes the recipe using 6 cups of pineapple juice. How many cups of orange juice and cups of soda water does he use? Explain.

25. The graph at the right represents the distance John runs in a race. Use the graph to describe John's progress during the course of the race. Does he run at a constant rate during the race? Explain.

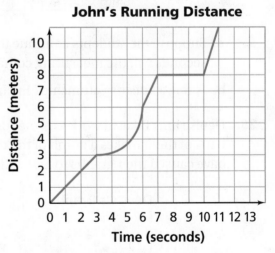

John's Running Distance

26. a. Does this graph represent a linear relationship? Explain.

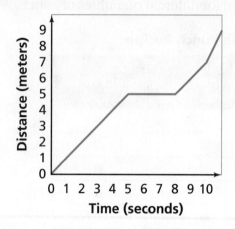

b. Could this graph represent a walking pattern? Explain.

For Exercises 27–29, students conduct an experiment to investigate the rate at which a leaking faucet loses water. They fill a paper cup with water, make a small hole in the bottom, and collect the dripping water in a measuring container, measuring the amount of water in the container at the end of each 10-second interval.

27. Students conducting the leaking-faucet experiment produce the table below. The measuring container they use has a capacity of 100 milliliters.

Leaking Faucet Experiment

Time (seconds)	10	20	30	40	50	60	70
Water Loss (milliliters)	2	5	8.5	11.5	14	16.5	19.5

a. Suppose the students continue their experiment. After how many seconds will the measuring container overflow?

b. Is this a linear relationship? Explain.

28. Denise and Takashi work together on the leaking-faucet experiment. Each of them makes a graph of the data they collect. What might have caused their graphs to look different?

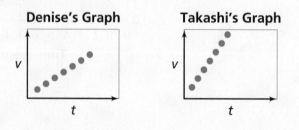

29. What might the graph below represent in the leaking-faucet experiment?

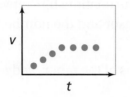

Extensions

30. a. The table below shows the populations of four cities for the past eight years. Describe how the population of each city changed over the eight years.

City Populations

Year	Population			
	Deep Valley	Nowhere	Swampville	Mount Silicon
0 (start)	1,000	1,000	1,000	1,000
1	1,500	900	1,500	2,000
2	2,000	800	2,500	4,000
3	2,500	750	3,000	8,000
4	3,000	700	5,000	16,000
5	3,500	725	3,000	32,000
6	4,000	900	2,500	64,000
7	4,500	1,500	1,500	128,000
8	5,000	1,700	1,000	256,000

b. Use the table to determine which relationships are linear.

c. Graph the data for each city. Describe how you selected ranges of values for the variables on the horizontal and vertical axes.

d. What are the advantages of using a table or a graph to represent the data?

31. In the walkathon, José asks his sponsors to donate $10 for the first 5 kilometers he walks and $1 per kilometer after 5 kilometers.

   a. Sketch a graph that represents the relationship between the money collected from each sponsor and the number of kilometers walked.

   b. Compare this graph to the graphs of the other pledge plans in Problem 1.3.

32. The cost C to make T-shirts for the walkathon is given by the equation $C = 20 + 5n$, where n is the number of T-shirts.

   a. Find the coordinates of a point that lies on the graph of this equation. Explain what information the coordinates represent in this context.

   b. Find the coordinates of a point above the line. Explain what information the coordinates represent in this context.

   c. Find the coordinates of a point below the line. Explain what information the coordinates represent in this context.

33. Reggie is looking forward to walking in a walkathon. He writes some equations to use to answer some questions he has about the walkathon. For each of parts (a)–(c), do the following two things:

   - Tell what information you think he was trying to find with the equation.

   - Write one question he could use the equation to answer.

   a. $y = 3x + 20$

   b. $y = 0.25x$

   c. $y = 4x$

Mathematical Reflections

In this Investigation, you began to explore linear relationships. You examined the patterns of change between two variables. The following questions will help you summarize what you have learned.

Think about these questions. Discuss your ideas with other students and your teacher. Then write a summary of your findings in your notebook.

1. **Describe** how the dependent variable changes as the independent variable changes in a linear relationship. Give examples.

2. **How** does the pattern of change between two variables in a linear relationship show up in

   a. a contextual situation?

   b. a table?

   c. a graph?

   d. an equation?

Common Core Mathematical Practices

As you worked on the Problems in this Investigation, you used prior knowledge to make sense of them. You also applied Mathematical Practices to solve the Problems. Think back over your work, the ways you thought about the Problems, and how you used Mathematical Practices.

Elena described her thoughts in the following way:

> At the end of Problem 1.3, we noticed that the linear relationship with the greatest positive pattern of change had the steepest line. For example, $A_{Gilberto} = 2n$ and $A_{Alana} = 5 + 0.5n$. The line of Gilberto's equation is steeper since it has a greater rate of change.
>
> This makes sense since as the number of kilometers increases by one unit, the money each sponsor donates to Gilberto increases by $2. The money each sponsor donates to Alana increases by $.50.
>
> For Leanne, the equation is $A_{Leanne} = 10$, so the change is 0. As the number of kilometers increases by one unit, the money each sponsor donates to Leanne does not change. The graph is a horizontal line.
>
> ....
>
> **Common Core Standards for Mathematical Practice**
>
> **MP8** Look for and express regularity in repeated reasoning.

? • What other Mathematical Practices can you identify in Elena's reasoning?

• Describe a Mathematical Practice that you and your classmates used to solve a different Problem in this Investigation.

Exploring Linear Relationships With Graphs and Tables

In the last Investigation, you examined linear relationships. For example, the distance, d, a person walks at a constant rate depends on the amount of time, t, the person walks. Also, the amount of money, A, a person raises from each sponsor depends on the distance, d, walked in the walkathon. Both of these relationships are linear. You might have written the following equations to represent these two relationships for Alana.

$$d = 1t$$
$$\text{and}$$
$$A = 5 + 0.5\,d$$

In this Investigation, you will continue to solve problems involving walking rates and other linear relationships.

Common Core State Standards

7.RP.A.2b Identify the constant of proportionality (unit rate) in tables, graphs, equations, diagrams, and verbal descriptions of proportional relationships.

7.RP.A.2c Represent proportional relationships by equations.

7.EE.B.3 Solve multi-step real-life and mathematical problems posed with positive and negative rational numbers in any form (whole numbers, fractions, and decimals), using tools strategically. Apply properties of operations to calculate with numbers in any form; convert between forms as appropriate; and assess the reasonableness of answers using mental computation and estimation strategies.

7.EE.B.4 Use variables to represent quantities in a real-world or mathematical problem, and construct simple equations and inequalities to solve problems by reasoning about the quantities.

Also 7.RP.A.2d, 7.EE.B.4a

2.1 Henri and Emile's Race
Finding the Point of Intersection

 In Ms. Chang's class, Emile found out that his walking rate is 2.5 meters per second. That is, Emile walks 2.5 meters every 1 second. When he gets home from school, he times his little brother Henri as Henri walks 100 meters. He figures out that Henri's walking rate is 1 meter per second. Henri walks 1 meter every second.

Problem 2.1

Henri challenges Emile to a walking race. Because Emile's walking rate is faster, Emile gives Henri a 45-meter head start. Emile knows his brother would enjoy winning the race, but he does not want to make the race so short that it is obvious his brother will win.

A How long should the race be so that Henri will win in a close race?

B Describe your strategy for finding your answer to Question A. Give evidence to support your answer.

 Homework starts on page 38.

2.2 Crossing the Line
Using Tables, Graphs, and Equations

Your class may have found some very interesting strategies for solving Problem 2.1, such as:

- Making a table showing time and distance data for both brothers

- Graphing time and distance data for both brothers on the same set of axes

- Writing an equation for each brother representing the relationship between time and distance

? How can each of these strategies be used to solve the Problem?

Problem 2.2

Ⓐ For each brother in Problem 2.1:

1. Make a table showing the distance from the starting line at several different times during the first 40 seconds. How can the table be used to find the length of the race?

2. Graph the time and the distance from the starting line on the same set of axes. How can the graph be used to find the length of the race?

3. Write an equation representing the relationship between time and distance. Explain what information each variable and number represents.

4. How does the walking rate of each brother show up in the graph, the table, and the equation?

Ⓑ 1. How far does Emile walk in 20 seconds?

2. After 20 seconds, how far apart are the brothers? How is this distance represented in the table and on the graph?

3. Is the point (26, 70) on either graph?

4. When will Emile overtake Henri? Explain.

Ⓒ How can you determine which of two lines will be steeper from

1. a table of the data?

2. an equation?

Ⓓ 1. At what points do Emile's and Henri's graphs cross the *y*-axis?

2. What information do these points represent in terms of the race?

3. How can these points be found in a table? In an equation?

 Homework starts on page 38.

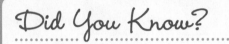

Did You Know?

Have you ever seen a walking race? You may have thought the walking style of the racers seemed rather strange. Race walkers must follow two rules:

• The walker must always have one foot in contact with the ground.

• The walker's leg must be straight from the time it strikes the ground until it passes under the body.

A champion race walker can cover a mile in about 6.5 minutes. It takes most people 15 to 20 minutes to walk a mile.

2.3 Comparing Costs
Comparing Relationships

All of the linear relationships you have studied so far can be written in the form $y = mx + b$, or $y = b + mx$. In this equation, y depends on x.

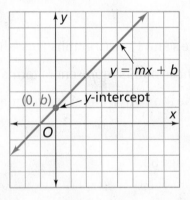

In Problem 2.2, you found the points at which Emile's and Henri's graphs cross the y-axis. These points are called the *y-intercepts*. The **y-intercept** is the point where the line crosses the y-axis, or when $x = 0$. The coordinates of the y-intercept for the graph shown above are $(0, b)$. To save time, we sometimes refer to the number b, rather than the coordinates of the point $(0, b)$, as the y-intercept.

A **coefficient** is the number that multiplies a variable in an equation. The m in $y = mx + b$ is the coefficient of x, so mx means m times x.

- You can represent the distance d_{Emile} that Emile walks after t seconds with the equation, $d_{Emile} = 2.5t$. The y-intercept is $(0, 0)$, and the coefficient of t is 2.5. You multiply Emile's walking rate by the time t he walks. He starts at a distance of 0 meters.

Emile

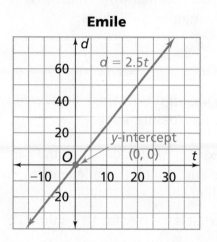

- You can represent the distance d_{Henri} that Henri is from where Emile started with the equation, $d_{Henri} = 45 + t$, where t is the time in seconds. The y-intercept is $(0, 45)$, and the coefficient of t is 1.

Henri

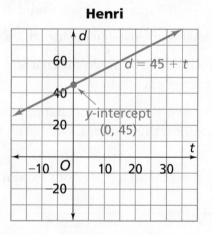

A **solution of an equation** is an ordered pair that makes the equation true and lies on the graph of the line.

- Is $(0, 45)$ a solution of the equation $d_{Henri} = 45 + t$? Explain.

- What would t be if $(t, 48)$ is a solution? Explain.

- What would d be if $(10, d)$ is a solution? Explain.

In this Problem, you will look at situations represented by an equation or a table.

Problem 2.3

Ms. Chang's class decides to give T-shirts to each person who participates in the walkathon. They receive bids for the cost of the T-shirts from two different companies. Mighty Tee charges $49 plus $1 per T-shirt. No-Shrink Tee charges $4.50 per T-shirt. Ms. Chang writes the following equations to represent the relationships relating cost to the number of T-shirts:

$$C_{Mighty} = 49 + n$$

$$C_{No-Shrink} = 4.5n$$

The number of T-shirts is n. C_{Mighty} is the cost in dollars for Mighty Tee. $C_{No-Shrink}$ is the cost in dollars for No-Shrink Tee.

Ⓐ **1.** For each equation, explain what information the y-intercept and the coefficient of n represent. What is the independent variable? What is the dependent variable?

2. For each company, what is the cost for 12 T-shirts? For 20 T-shirts?

3. Lani calculates that the school has about $120 to spend on T-shirts. From which company will $120 buy the most T-shirts? Explain your answer.

4. a. For what number of T-shirts is the cost of the two companies equal? What is that cost? Explain how you found the answers.

   b. How can this information be used to decide which plan to choose?

5. a. Explain why the relationship between the cost and the number of T-shirts for each company is linear.

   b. In each equation, what is the pattern of change between the two variables? That is, by how much does C change for every 1 unit that n increases?

   c. How is this situation similar to the previous two Problems?

Problem **2.3** *continued*

B The following table represents the costs from another company, The Big T.

T-Shirt Costs

n	C
0	34
3	41.5
5	46.5
8	54
10	59

1. Compare the costs for this company to the costs for the two companies in Question A.

2. Is the relationship between the two variables in this plan linear? If so, what is the pattern of change between the two variables?

3. **a.** Would the point (20, 84) lie on the graph of this cost plan? Explain.

   b. What information about the number of T-shirts and cost do the coordinates of the point (20, 84) represent?

   c. What equation relates C and n?

   d. Would (20, 80) be a solution of the equation? Would (14, 69) be a solution? Explain.

A C E Homework starts on page 38.

2.4 Connecting Tables, Graphs, and Equations

 Look again at Alana's pledge plan from Problem 1.3. Suppose A represents the amount raised in dollars and d represents the distance walked in kilometers. You can express this plan with the equation $A = 5 + 0.5d$.

Alana's Pledge Plan

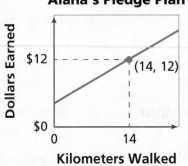

- Explain why the point (14, 12) is on the graph of Alana's pledge plan.

- Write a question you could answer by locating this point.

- How can you use the equation for Alana's pledge plan to check the answer to the question you made up?

- How can you use a graph to find the number of kilometers that Alana walks if a sponsor donates $17? How could you use an equation to answer this question?

In this Problem, you will investigate similar questions relating to pledge plans for a walkathon.

Problem 2.4

Consider the following pledge plans. In each equation, y is the amount pledged in dollars by each sponsor, and x is the distance walked in kilometers.

Plan 1	Plan 2	Plan 3
$y = 5x - 3$	$y = -x + 6$	$y = 2$

*Problem*2.4 *continued*

A For each pledge plan:

 1. What information does the equation give about the pledge plan? Does the plan make sense?

 2. Make a table of values of x from -5 to 5.

 3. Sketch a graph of the relationship. What part of each graph is relevant to the situation?

 4. Do the y-values increase, decrease, or stay the same as the x-values increase? Explain how you can find the answer using a table, a graph, or an equation.

B **1.** Which graph from Question A, part (3) contains the point $(2, 4)$?

 2. How do the coordinates $(2, 4)$ relate to the equation of the line? To the corresponding table of data?

 3. Write a question you could answer by locating this point.

C **1.** Which relationship has a graph you can use to find the value of x that makes $8 = 5x - 3$ a true statement?

 2. How does finding the value of x in $8 = 5x - 3$ help you find the coordinates for a point on the graph of the relationship?

D The following three points all lie on the graph of the same plan:

$$(-7, 13) \qquad (1.2, \blacksquare) \qquad (\blacksquare, -4)$$

 1. Two of the points have a missing coordinate. Find the missing coordinate. Explain how you found it.

 2. Write a question you could answer by finding the missing coordinate.

E **1.** Describe how a point on a graph is related to a table and an equation that represent the same relationship.

 2. How can you use a table, a graph, or an equation that represents the relationship $y = 5x - 3$ to

 a. find the value of y when $x = 7$?

 b. find the value of x when $y = 23$?

A C E Homework starts on page 38.

Applications

1. Grace and Allie are going to meet at the fountain near their houses. They both leave their houses at the same time. Allie passes Grace's house on her way to the fountain.

   - Allie's walking rate is 2 meters per second.
   - Grace's walking rate is 1.5 meters per second.

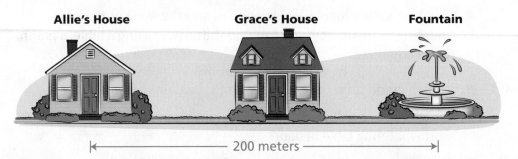

Allie's House   Grace's House   Fountain

|← —————————— 200 meters —————————— →|

   a. How many seconds will it take Allie to reach the fountain?

   b. Suppose Grace's house is 90 meters from the fountain. Who will reach the fountain first, Allie or Grace? Explain your reasoning.

2. In Problem 2.2, Emile's friend, Gilberto, joins the race. Gilberto has a head start of 20 meters and walks at 2 meters per second.

   a. Write an equation that gives the relationship between Gilberto's distance d from where Emile starts and the time t.

   b. How would Gilberto's graph compare to Emile's and Henri's graphs?

3. Ingrid stops at Tara's house on her way to school. Tara's mother says that Tara left 5 minutes ago. Ingrid leaves Tara's house, walking quickly to catch up with Tara. The graph below shows the distance each girl is from Tara's house, starting from the time Ingrid leaves Tara's house.

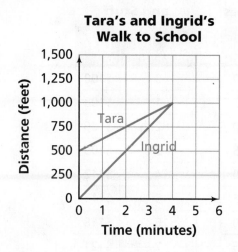

a. In what way is this situation like the race between Henri and Emile? In what way is it different?

b. After how many minutes does Ingrid catch up with Tara?

c. How far from Tara's house does Ingrid catch up with Tara?

d. Each graph intersects the distance axis (the *y*-axis). What information do these points of intersection give about the situation?

e. Which line is steeper? How can you tell from the graph? How is the steepness of each line related to the rate at which the person travels?

f. What do you think the graphs would look like if we extended them to show distance and time after the girls meet?

In Exercises 4 and 5, the student council asks for cost estimates for a skating party to celebrate the end of the school year.

4. The following tables represent the costs from two skating companies.

Rollaway Skates

Number of People	Cost
0	$0
1	$5
2	$10
3	$15
4	$20
5	$25
6	$30
7	$35
8	$40

Wheelie's Skates and Stuff

Number of People	Cost
0	$100
1	$103
2	$106
3	$109
4	$112
5	$115
6	$118
7	$121
8	$124

a. For each company, is the relationship between the number of people and cost a linear relationship? Explain.

b. For each company, write an equation that represents the relationship between the cost and the number of people. What is the dependent variable? What is the independent variable?

c. Describe how you can use the table or a graph to find when the costs of the two plans are equal. How can this information help the student council decide which company to choose?

5. A third company, Wheels to Go, gives their quote in the form of the equation $C_W = 35 + 4n$, where C_W is the cost in dollars for n students.

a. What information do the numbers 35 and 4 represent in this situation?

b. For 60 students, which of the three companies is the cheapest? Explain how you could determine the answer using tables, graphs, or equations.

c. Suppose the student council wants to keep the cost of the skating party to $500. How many people can they invite under each of the three plans?

d. The points below lie on one or more of the graphs of the three cost plans. Decide to which plan(s) each point belongs.

   i. (20, 115)   **ii.** (65, 295)   **iii.** (50, 250)

e. Pick one of the points in part (d). Write a question that could be answered by locating this point.

6. A band decides to sell protein bars to raise money for an upcoming trip. The cost (the amount the band pays for the protein bars) and the income the band receives for the protein bars are represented on the graph.

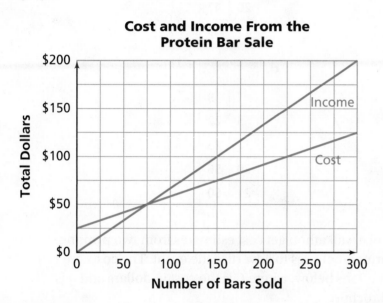

a. How many protein bars must be sold for the cost to equal the income?

b. What is the income from selling 50 protein bars? 125 bars?

c. Suppose the income is $200. How many protein bars were sold? How much of this income is profit?

7. Suppose each of the following patterns continues.

   - Which represent linear relationships? Explain your answer.

   - For those that are linear relationships, write an equation that expresses the relationship.

a.

x	y
−10	−29
0	1
10	31
20	61
30	91

b.

x	y
1	9
5	17
7	21
20	47
21	49

c.

x	y
1	1
2	4
3	9
4	16
5	25

d.

x	y
1	9
5	22
7	25
20	56
21	60

8. The organizers of a walkathon get cost estimates from two printing companies to print brochures to advertise the event. The costs are given by the equations below, where C is the cost in dollars and n is the number of brochures.

Company A	Company B
$C = 15 + 0.10n$	$C = 0.25n$

   a. For what number of brochures are the costs the same for both companies? What method did you use to get your answer?

   b. The organizers have $65 to spend on brochures. How many brochures can they have printed if they use Company A? If they use Company B?

   c. What information does the y-intercept of the graph represent for each equation?

   d. What information does the coefficient of n represent for each equation?

   e. For each company, describe the change in the cost as the number of brochures increases by 1.

9. A school committee is assigned the task of selecting a DJ for the end-of-school-year party. Darius obtains several quotes for the cost of three DJs.

Compare DJs

$60 per hour

$100 set-up fee
plus
$40 per hour

$175 set-up fee
plus
$30 per hour

   a. For each DJ, write an equation that shows how the total cost *C* relates to the number of hours *x*.

   b. What information does the coefficient of *x* represent for each DJ?

   c. For each DJ, what information does the *y*-intercept of the graph represent?

   d. Suppose the DJ will need to work eight and one half hours. What is the cost of each DJ?

   e. Suppose the committee has only $450 dollars to spend on a DJ. For how many hours could each DJ play?

10. A local department store offers two installment plans for buying a $270 skateboard.

> **Plan 1** A fixed weekly payment of $10.80
>
> **Plan 2** A $120 initial payment plus $6.00 per week

   a. For each plan, how much money is owed after 12 weeks?

   b. Which plan requires the least number of weeks to pay for the skateboard? Explain.

   c. Write an equation for each plan. Explain what information the variables and numbers represent.

   d. Suppose the skateboard costs $355. How would the answers to parts (a)–(c) change?

For each equation in Exercises 11–14, answer parts (a)–(d).

   a. What is the rate of change?

   b. State whether the y-values are increasing, decreasing, or neither as x increases.

   c. Give the y-intercept.

   d. List the coordinates of two points that lie on the graph of the equation.

11. $y = 1.5x$

12. $y = -3x + 10$

13. $y = -2x + 6$

14. $y = 2x + 5$

15. Dani earns \$7.50 per hour when she babysits.

   a. Draw a graph that relates the number of hours she babysits and the total amount of money she earns.

   b. Choose a point on the graph. Ask two questions that can be answered by finding the coordinates of this point.

16. Martel wants to use his calculator to find the value of x when $y = 22$ in the equation $y = 100 - 3x$. Explain how he can use each table or graph to find the value of x when $100 - 3x = 22$.

a.

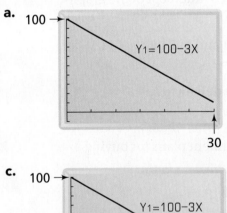

b.

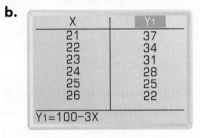

c.

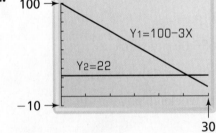

17. Match each equation to a graph.

    a. $y = 3x + 5$ **b.** $y = x - 7$ **c.** $y = -x - 10$

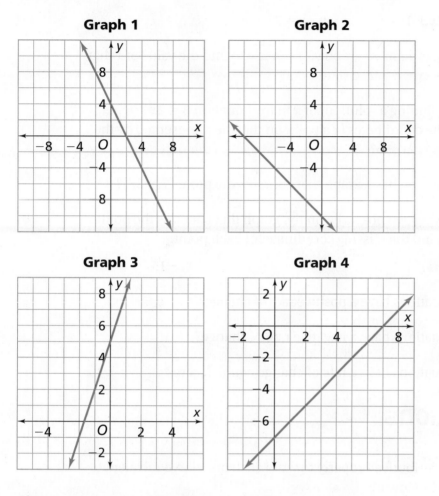

Graph 1

Graph 2

Graph 3

Graph 4

    d. Write an equation for the graph that has no match.

For each equation in Exercises 18–21, give two values for x for which the value of y is negative.

18. $y = -2x - 5$ **19.** $y = -5$

20. $y = 2x - 5$ **21.** $y = \frac{3}{2}x - \frac{1}{4}$

For Exercises 22–28, consider the following equations:

       i. $y = 2x$ **ii.** $y = -5x$ **iii.** $y = 2x - 6$

      iv. $y = -2x + 1$ **v.** $y = 7$

22. Which equation has a graph you can use to find the value of x that makes $8 = 2x - 6$ a true statement?

23. How does finding a solution for x in the equation $8 = 2x - 6$ help you find the coordinates of a point on the line represented by the equation $y = 2x - 6$?

24. Which equation has a graph that contains the point $(7, -35)$?

25. The following two points lie on the graph that contains the point $(7, -35)$. Find the missing coordinate for each point.

       $(-1.2, \blacksquare)$ $(\blacksquare, -15)$

26. Which equations have a positive rate of change?

27. Which equations have a negative rate of change?

28. Which equations have a rate of change equal to zero?

Connections

29. Use the Distributive Property to write an expression equivalent to each of the following:

    a. $x(-2 + 3)$ **b.** $(-4x) + (2x)$ **c.** $(x) - (4x)$

30. Decide whether each statement is true or false. Explain your reasoning.

    a. $15 - 3x = 15 + -3x$

    b. $3.5x + 5 = 5(0.7x + 5)$

    c. $3(2x + 1) = (2x + 1) + (2x + 1) + (2x + 1)$

31. The Ferry family decides to buy a new television that costs $215. The store has an installment plan that allows them to make a $35 down payment and then pay $15 a month. Use the graph to answer the questions below.

Paying for a TV on an Installment Plan

a. Write an equation that represents the relationship between the amount the Ferry family still owes and the number of months after the purchase. Explain what information the numbers and variables represent.

b. The point where the graph of an equation intersects the x-axis is called the **x-intercept**. What are the x- and y-intercepts of the graph for this payment plan? Explain what information each intercept represents.

32. Shallah Middle School is planning a school trip. The cost is $5 per person. The organizers know that three adults are going on the trip, but they do not yet know the number of students who will go. Write an expression that represents the total costs for x students and three adults.

33. Use the Distributive Property to write two expressions that show two different ways to compute the area of each rectangle.

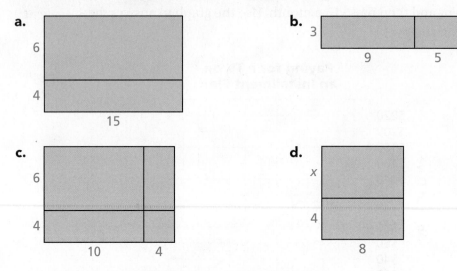

a.

6
4
15

b.

3
9   5

c.

6
4
10   4

d.

x
4
8

34. Harvest Foods has apples on sale at 12 for $3.

The Cost of Apples

Number of Apples	12	■	1	48	10	■
Cost	$3	$1.50	■	■	■	$4.50

  a. What is the cost per apple?

  b. Complete the rate table to show the costs of different numbers of apples.

  c. How many apples can you buy for $1?

  d. Is the relationship between number of apples and cost linear? Explain.

35. Lamar bought some bagels for his friends. He paid $15 for 20 bagels.

  a. How much did Lamar pay per bagel?

  b. Write an equation relating the number of bagels, *n*, to the total cost, *C*.

  c. Use your equation to find the cost of 150 bagels.

36. DeAndre says that $x = -1$ makes the equation $-8 = -3 + 5x$ true. Tamara checks this value for x in the equation. She says DeAndre is wrong because $-3 + 5 \times (-1)$ is -2, not -8. Why do you think these students disagree?

37. Determine whether the following mathematical sentences are true or false.

   a. $5 + 3 \times 2 = 16$ **b.** $3 \times 2 + 5 = 16$

   c. $5 + 3 \times 2 = 11$ **d.** $3 \times 2 + 5 = 11$

   e. $\frac{3}{2} \div \frac{4}{3} - \frac{1}{8} = 1$ **f.** $\frac{1}{2} + \frac{3}{2} \div \frac{1}{2} = 2$

38. Jamal feeds his dog the same amount of dog food each day from a very large bag. The number of cups left on the 3rd day and the number of cups left on the 11th day are shown below.

Day 3 — 44 cups — WOOF FOOD

Day 11 — 28 cups — WOOF FOOD

   a. How many cups of food does he feed his dog a day?

   b. How many cups of food were in the bag when he started?

   c. Write an equation for the total amount of dog food Jamal has left after feeding his dog for d days.

39. a. Match the following connecting paths for the last 5 minutes of Jalissa's race.

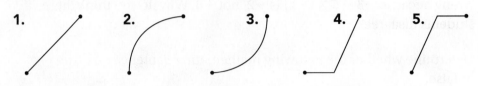

1.   2.   3.   4.   5.

    i. Jalissa finishes running at a constant rate.

   ii. Jalissa runs slowly at first and gradually increases her speed.

  iii. Jalissa runs quickly and then gradually decreases her speed.

  iv. Jalissa runs quickly and reaches the finish line early.

   v. After falling, Jalissa runs at a constant rate.

  b. Which of the situations in part (a) was most likely to represent Jalissa's running for the entire race? Explain your answer.

40. In *Stretching and Shrinking,* you plotted the points (8, 6), (8, 22), and (24, 14) on grid paper to form a triangle.

  a. Draw the triangle you get when you apply the rule $(0.5x, 0.5y)$ to the three points.

  b. Draw the triangle you get when you apply the rule $(0.25x, 0.25y)$ to the three points.

  c. How are the three triangles you have drawn related?

  d. What are the areas of the three triangles?

  e. Do you notice any linear relationships among the data of the three triangles, such as the area, scale factor, lengths of sides, and so on?

41. In *Covering and Surrounding,* you looked at perimeters of rectangles.

  a. Make a table of possible whole number values for the length and width of a rectangle with a perimeter of 20 meters.

  b. Write an equation that represents the data in this table. Make sure to define your variables.

  c. Is the relationship between length and width linear in this case? Explain.

  d. Find the area of each rectangle.

Extensions

42. For each equation below, decide whether it models a linear relationship. Explain how you decided.

   a. $y = 2x$ **b.** $y = \frac{2}{x}$ **c.** $y = x^2$

43. a. Write equations for three lines that intersect to form a triangle.

   b. Sketch the graphs and label the coordinates of the vertices of the triangle.

   c. Will any three lines intersect to form a triangle? Explain.

44. a. Which one of the following points is on the line $y = 3x - 7$: $(3, 3)$, $(3, 2)$, $(3, 1)$, or $(3, 0)$? Describe where each of the other three points is in relation to the line.

   b. Find another point on the line $y = 3x - 7$ and three more points above the line.

   c. The equation $y = 3x - 7$ is true for $(4, 5)$ and $(7, 14)$. Use this information to find two points that make the inequality $y < 3x - 7$ true and two points that make the inequality $y > 3x - 7$ true.

45. Ms. Chang's class decides to order posters that advertise the walkathon. Ichiro obtains quotes from two different companies.

> **Clear Prints** charges $2 per poster.

> **Posters by Sue** charges $15 plus $.50 per poster.

   a. For each company, write an equation Ichiro could use to calculate the cost for any number of posters.

   b. For what number of posters is the cost the same for both companies? Explain.

   c. Which company do you think the class should buy posters from? Explain your reasoning.

   d. If Ms. Chang's class has an $18 budget for posters, which company do you think the class should buy posters from? If Ms. Chang donates an additional $10 for ordering posters, does it impact the decision made? What factors influenced your decision?

   e. Use the information from parts (a)–(c) to find an ordered pair that makes the inequality $C < 20$ true for Clear Prints. Find an ordered pair that makes the inequality $C > 20$ true for Posters by Sue.

Mathematical Reflections 2

In this Investigation, you continued to explore patterns of change between the independent and dependent variables in a linear relationship. You learned how to use tables, graphs, and equations to solve problems that involve linear relationships. The following questions will help you summarize what you have learned.

Think about these questions. Discuss your ideas with other students and your teacher. Then write a summary of your findings in your notebook.

1. **a. Explain** how the information about a linear relationship is represented in a table, a graph, or an equation.

    b. Describe several real-world situations that can be modeled by equations of the form $y = mx + b$ or $y = mx$. Explain how the latter equation represents a proportional relationship.

2. **a. Explain** how a table or a graph that represents a linear relationship can be used to solve a problem.

    b. Explain how you have used an equation that represents a linear relationship to solve a problem.

Common Core Mathematical Practices

As you worked on the Problems in this Investigation, you used prior knowledge to make sense of them. You also applied Mathematical Practices to solve the Problems. Think back over your work, the ways you thought about the Problems, and how you used Mathematical Practices.

Tori described her thoughts in the following way:

> In Problem 2.1, we looked at how far apart the brothers were after t seconds. For example, at the start of the race, they are 45 meters apart. After 1 second, they are $45 - 1.5 = 43.5$ meters apart. After 2 seconds, they are 42 meters apart. After 10 seconds, they are 30 meters apart.
>
> We made a table and found the time it took for Emile to catch up to Henri, or when the distance between them is 0, which is 30 seconds. We used this to choose the length of the race so that Henri wins the race.
>
> Another group member made a graph of the data (time, distance apart), and we saw that it is a line that is decreasing. It started at the y-intercept of 45 meters and crossed the x-axis at 30 seconds.
>
> ....
>
> **Common Core Standards for Mathematical Practice**
> **MP2** Reason abstractly and quantitatively.

? • What other Mathematical Practices can you identify in Tori's reasoning?

• Describe a Mathematical Practice that you and your classmates used to solve a different Problem in this Investigation.

Solving Equations

In the last Investigation, you examined the patterns in the table and graph for the relationship relating Alana's distance d and money earned A in the walkathon.

The equation $A = 5 + 0.5d$ is another way to represent that relationship. The graph of the relationship is a line that contains infinitely many points. The coordinates of each point can be substituted into the equation to make a true statement. The coordinates of these points are solutions to the equation.

....

Common Core State Standards

7.EE.A.1 Apply properties of operations as strategies to add, subtract, factor, and expand linear expressions with rational coefficients.

7.EE.A.2 Understand that rewriting an expression in different forms in a problem context can shed light on the problem and how the quantities in it are related.

7.EE.B.4a Solve word problems leading to equations of the form $px + q = r$ and $p(x + q) = r$, where p, q, and r are specific rational numbers. Solve equations of these forms fluently. Compare an algebraic solution to an arithmetic solution, identifying the sequence of the operations used in each approach.

7.EE.B.4b Solve word problems leading to inequalities of the form $px + q > r$ or $px + q < r$, where p, q, and r are specific rational numbers. Graph the solution set of the inequality and interpret it in the context of the problem.

Also 7.EE.B.4

For example, the point (3, 6.5) lies on the line of $A = 5 + 0.5d$. This means that $d = 3$, $A = 6.5$, and $6.5 = 5 + 0.5(3)$ is a true statement. So, the coordinate pair (3, 6.5) is a solution to the equation.

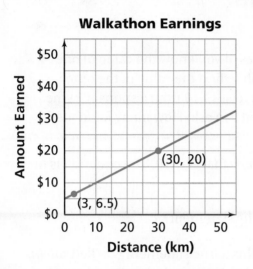

Walkathon Earnings

- Does the point (30, 20) lie on the line? Is it a solution to the equation? Explain.

- Does the point (20, 20) lie on the line? Is it a solution to the equation? Explain.

- What happens if you choose a point that is not visible on this section of the graph, such as (70, 40)? Is it on the line? Explain.

The corresponding entries in a table are the coordinates of points on the line representing the equation $A = 5 + 0.5d$. So, we can also find a solution to an equation by using a table.

- How could you find the value of d that corresponds to $A = 30$ in the table?

d	A
0	5
1	5.5
2	6
3	6.5
4	7
20	15
25	17.5
30	20

3.1 Solving Equations Using Tables and Graphs

In a relationship between two variables, if you know the value of one variable, you can use a table or a graph to find the value of the other variable. For example, suppose Alana raises $10 from a sponsor in the walkathon from Problem 1.3. Then you can ask: How many kilometers does Alana walk?

In the equation $A = 5 + 0.5d$, this means that $A = 10$. The equation is now $10 - 5 + 0.5d$.

- What value of d will make this a true statement?

Finding the value of d that will make this a true statement is called *solving the equation* for d. You can use tables or graphs to find the missing value. In this Investigation, you will develop strategies for solving equations symbolically, using properties of operations and equality.

Problem 3.1

A Use the equation $A = 5 + 0.5d$.

1. a. Suppose Alana walks 23 kilometers. Show how you can use a table and a graph to find the amount of money each sponsor donates.

b. Write an equation that represents the amount of money Alana collects if she walks 23 kilometers. Can you use the equation to find the amount? Explain.

2. Suppose Alana writes the equation $30 = 5 + 0.5d$.

a. What question is she trying to ask?

b. Show how you can answer Alana's question by reasoning with a table of values, a graph of the relationship $A = 5 + 0.5d$, or with the equation $30 = 5 + 0.5d$ itself.

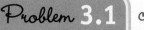 **Problem 3.1** continued

B The equation $D = 25 + 2.5t$ is related to situations that you have explored. In parts (1) and (2) below, the value of one variable in the equation is known. Find the solution (the value of the unknown variable) in each part. Then, describe another way you can find the solution.

  1. $D = 25 + 2.5(7)$ **2.** $70 = 25 + 2.5t$

A C E Homework starts on page 69.

3.2 Mystery Pouches in the Kingdom of Montarek
Exploring Equality

In the Kingdom of Montarek, money takes the form of $1 gold coins called rubas. Messengers carry money between the king's castles in sealed pouches that always hold equal numbers of coins.

$1 gold coin   sealed pouch

One day a messenger arrived at one of the castles with a box containing two sealed pouches and five loose $1 coins. The ruler thanked the messenger for the money, which equaled $11.

• Can you figure out the number of coins in each pouch?

• Does the following visual equation help in finding the number of coins in each pouch?

In this Problem, you will solve more problems involving mystery pouches.

Problem 3.2

A In parts (1)–(6) below, each pouch contains the same number of $1 gold coins. Also, the total number of coins on each side of the equation is the same.

- Find the number of gold coins in each pouch. Write down your steps so that someone else could follow your steps to find the number of coins in a pouch.

- Describe how you can check your answer. That is, how do you know you have found the correct number of gold coins in each pouch?

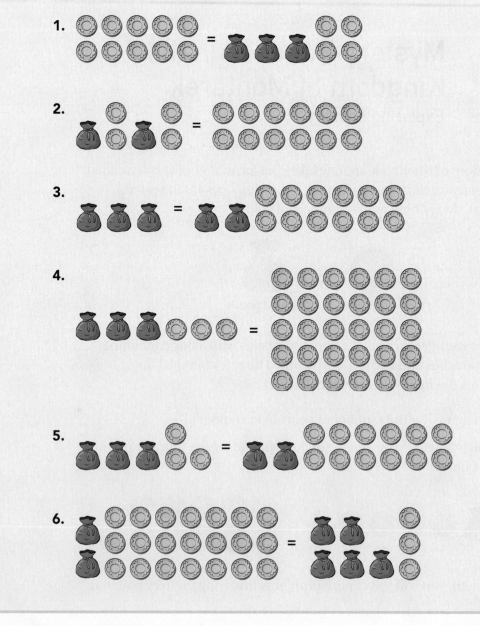

Problem 3.2 *continued*

B In Question A, part (2), Nichole thought of the left-hand side of the situation as having two groups. Each group contained one pouch and two coins. She visualized the following steps to help her find the number of coins in a pouch.

1. Is Nichole correct? Explain.

2. Noah looked at Nichole's strategy and claimed that she was applying the Distributive Property. Is Noah's claim correct? Explain.

3. Are there other situations in which Nichole's method might work? Explain.

A C E Homework starts on page 69.

3.3 From Pouches to Variables
Writing Equations

In the last Problem, you used pictures of pouches and gold coins to solve equations. Your solutions maintained the equality of the coins on both sides of the equal sign. For example, you might have removed (or subtracted) the same number of coins or pouches from each side of the equation. To better understand how to maintain equality, let's look first at numerical statements.

The equation $85 = 70 + 15$ states that the quantities 85 and $70 + 15$ are equal.

What do you have to do to maintain equality if you:

- subtract 15 from the left-hand side of the original equation?

- add 10 to the right-hand side of the original equation?

- divide the left-hand side of the original equation by 5?

- multiply the right-hand side of the original equation by 4?

Try your methods on another example of equality. Summarize what you know about maintaining equality between two quantities.

Throughout this Unit, you have been solving equations with two variables. Sometimes the value of one variable is known, and you want to find the value of the other variable. In this Problem, you will continue to find the value of a variable without using a table or a graph. You will learn to use *symbolic* methods to solve a linear equation.

The picture below shows a situation from Problem 3.2.

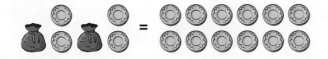

Because the number of gold coins in each pouch is unknown, you can let *x* represent the number of coins in one pouch. You can let 1 represent the value of one gold coin.

You can write the following equation to represent the situation:

$$2x + 4 = 12$$

Or, you can use Nichole's method from Problem 3.2 to write this equation:

$$2(x + 2) = 12$$

The expressions $2x + 4$ and $2(x + 2)$ are **equivalent expressions.** Two or more expressions are equivalent if they have the same value, regardless of what number is substituted for the variable. These two expressions are an example of the Distributive Property for numbers.

$$2(x + 2) = 2x + 4$$

In this Problem, you will revisit situations with pouches and coins, but you will use symbolic equations to represent your solution process.

Problem 3.3

Ⓐ For each situation, find the number of coins in each pouch. Record your answers in a table like the one shown.

Picture	Steps for Finding the Coins in Each Pouch	Solution Using Equations
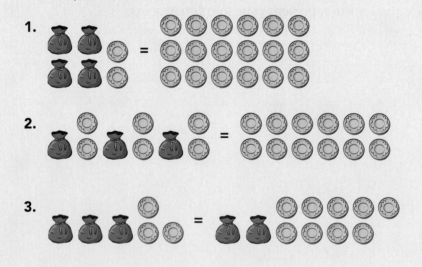		

- In the second column, use your method from Problem 3.2 to find the number of gold coins in each pouch. Record your steps.

- In the third column, write an equation that represents the situation. Use *x* to represent the number of gold coins in each pouch. Use the number 1 to represent each coin. Then, use your equation to find the number of gold coins in each pouch.

- Check your answers.

1.

2.

3.

Problem **3.3**   *continued*

4.

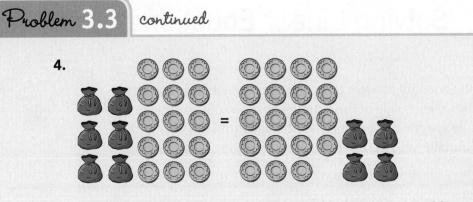

5. Describe two situations in Question A for which you could write more than one equation to represent the situation.

B For each equation:

- Use your strategies from Question A to solve the equation.

- Check your answer.

  1. $30 = 6 + 4x$

  2. $7x = 5 + 5x$

  3. $7x + 2 = 12 + 5x$

  4. $2(x + 4) = 16$

C Describe a general method for solving equations using what you know about equality.

A C E Homework starts on page 69.

3.4 Solving Linear Equations

To maintain the equality of two expressions, you can add, subtract, multiply, or divide each side of the equality by the same number. These are called the **properties of equality**. In the last Problem, you applied properties of equality and numbers to find a solution to an equation.

So far in this Investigation, all of the situations have involved positive whole numbers.

- Does it make sense to think about negative numbers in a coin situation?

- Does it make sense to think about fractions in a coin situation?

> **?** What strategies do you have for solving an equation like $-2x + 10 = 15$?

You have used the properties of equality to solve equations involving pouches and coins. These properties are also useful in solving all linear equations.

Problem 3.4

A For parts 1–3:

- Record each step you take to find your solution.

- Then, check your answer.

1. **a.** $5x + 10 = 20$ **b.** $5x - 10 = 20$ **c.** $5x + 10 = -20$

   d. $5x - 10 = -20$ **e.** $10 - 5x = 20$ **f.** $10 - 5x = -20$

2. **a.** $\frac{1}{4}x + 6 = 12$ **b.** $1\frac{1}{2} + 2x = 6\frac{1}{2}$ **c.** $\frac{3}{5} = -x + 1$

   d. $3.5x = 130 + 10x$ **e.** $15 - 4x = 10x + 45$

3. **a.** $3(x + 1) = 21$ **b.** $2 + 3(x + 1) = 6x$ **c.** $-2(2x - 3) = -2$

Problem 3.4 continued

B Below are examples of students' solutions the equations from Question A, part (3) above. Is each solution correct? If not, explain what the error is.

$$3(x + 1) = 21$$

Corry's Solution

3 times something in the parentheses must be 21.
So 3( ) = 21.
The something is 7.
So x + 1 = 7, and
x = 6.

$$2 + 3(x + 1) = 6x$$

Hadden's Solution

2 + 3(x + 1) is equivalent to 5(x + 1).
So I can rewrite the original equation as 5(x + 1) = 6x.
Using the Distributive Property, this is the same as
　　5x + 5 = 6x.
Subtracting 5x from each side, I get 5 = 1x.
So x = 5.

$$-2(2x - 3) = -2$$

Jackie's Solution

By using the Distributive Property on the left-hand
　　side of the equality, I get −4x − 6 = −2.
By adding 6 to each side, I get −4x = 4.
By dividing both sides by −4, I get x = −1.

C Describe the strategies you have used for solving linear equations. When might you use one over another?

A C E Homework starts on page 69.

3.5 Finding the Point of Intersection
Equations and Inequalities

In Problem 2.3, you used graphs and tables to find when the costs of two different plans for buying T-shirts were equal. The graphs of the two cost plans are shown below. C_n represents the costs of the No-Shrink Tee. C_m represents the costs of the Mighty Tee. The **point of intersection** of the two lines tells us when the costs for the two T-shirt plans are equal.

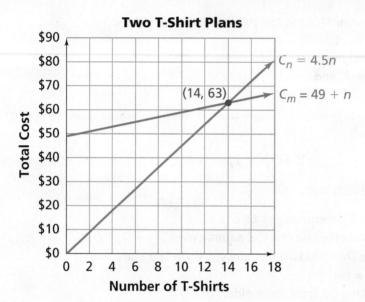

Two T-Shirt Plans

$C_n = 4.5n$

$C_m = 49 + n$

(14, 63)

Total Cost: $90, $80, $70, $60, $50, $40, $30, $20, $10, $0

Number of T-Shirts: 0, 2, 4, 6, 8, 10, 12, 14, 16, 18

- What information do the coordinates of the point of intersection of the two lines give you about this situation?

- Show how you could use the two equations to find the coordinates of the point of intersection of the two lines. That is, for what number of T-shirts n is $C_m = C_n$?

- For what number(s) of T-shirts is plan C_m less than plan C_n? That is, when is $C_m < C_n$?

Statements like $C_m = C_n$ are called equality statements or equations. You learned how to solve these equations symbolically in this Investigation.

Statements like $C_m < C_n$, $x < 5$, and $x > -5$ are called **inequality statements** or inequalities.

In this Problem, you will answer questions about points of intersection and about when the cost of one plan is less than or greater than that of another plan.

Problem 3.5

At Fabulous Fabian's Bakery, the expenses E to make n cakes per month is given by the equation $E = 825 + 3.25n$. The income I for selling n cakes is given by the equation $I = 8.20n$.

A **1.** In the equations for I and E, what information do the y-intercepts give you?

2. What do the coefficients of n represent?

B Fabian sells 100 cakes in January.

1. What are his expenses and his income?

2. What is his profit? Describe how you found your answer.

3. Kevin drew the graph below. Explain how he could use his graph to determine Fabian's profit.

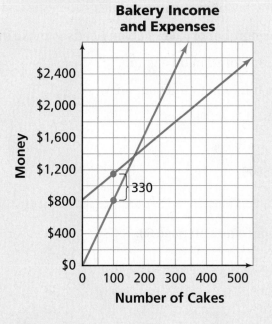

Bakery Income and Expenses

C **1.** Write an equation that represents the profit, P, for selling n cakes. Describe how you can use this equation to find the profit.

2. Fabian uses the equation $P = 4.95n - 825$ to predict the profit. Does this equation make sense? Explain.

continued on the next page >

Problem 3.5 *continued*

D The *break-even* point is when expenses equal income ($E = I$). Fabian thinks that this information is useful.

1. Write an equation to find the number of cakes n needed to break even. How many cakes does Fabian need to make in order to break even?

2. Describe how you could use a table or graph to find the break-even point.

E **1.** How many cakes can Fabian make if he wants his expenses to be less than $2,400 a month?

2. How many cakes can he make if he wants to his income to be greater than $2,400 a month?

3. Fabian's sister Mariah wrote the following inequality statements to answer parts (1) and (2) above.

$$825 + 3.25n < 2,400 \quad \text{and} \quad 8.20n > 2,400$$

Do these statements make sense? Why?

4. For each of the following inequalities

- find the number of cakes Fabian needs to make in a month.

- record the solution on a graph.

- explain how you found your answers.

a. $E < 1,475$

b. $I > 1,640$

c. $P > 800$

A C E Homework starts on page 69.

Applications

1. Ms. Chang's class decides to use the *Cool Tee's* company to make their T-shirts. The following equation represents the relationship between the cost C and the number of T-shirts n.

$$C = 2n + 20$$

   a. The class wants to buy 25 T-shirts from *Cool Tee's*. Describe how you can use a table and a graph to find the cost for 25 T-shirts.

   b. Suppose the class has $80 to spend on T-shirts. Describe how you can use a table and a graph to find the number of T-shirts the class can buy.

   c. Taleah writes the following equation in her notebook:

$$C = 2(15) + 20$$

   What information is Sophia looking for?

   d. Keisha uses the coordinates (30, 80) to find information about the cost of the T-shirts. What information is she looking for?

2. Mary uses the following equations to find some information about three walkathon pledge plans.

Plan 1	**Plan 2**	**Plan 3**
$14 = 2x$	$y = 3.5(10) + 10$	$100 = 1.5x + 55$

   In each equation, y is the amount donated in dollars, and x is the number of kilometers walked. For each equation:

   a. What information is Mary trying to find?

   b. Describe how you could find the information.

3. Find the solution (the value of the variable) for each equation.

   a. $y = 3(10) + 15$ b. $24 = x + 2$ c. $10 = 2x + 4$

4. Consider the equation $y = 5x - 15$.

   a. Find y if $x = 1$.   b. Find x if $y = 50$.

   c. Describe how you can use a table or a graph to answer parts (a) and (b).

For each situation in Exercises 5–8, find the number of coins in each pouch. Each pouch contains the same number of $1 gold coins, and the total number of coins on each side of the equation is the same.

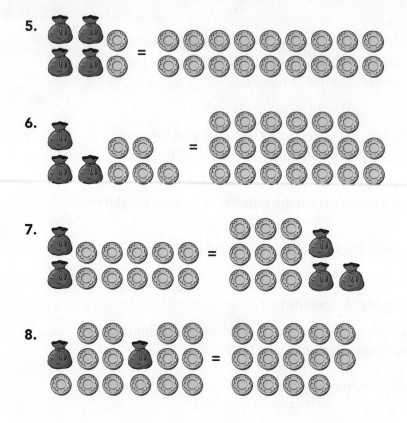

5.

6.

7.

8.

9. For each equation, sketch a picture using pouches and coins. Then, determine how many coins are in a pouch.

   a. $3x = 12$

   b. $2x + 5 = 19$

   c. $4x + 5 = 2x + 19$

   d. $x + 12 = 2x + 6$

   e. $3(x + 4) = 18$

10. Gilberto's grandfather gives him $5 for his birthday and then 50¢ for each math question he answers correctly on his math exams for the year.

   a. Write an equation that represents the amount of money that Gilberto receives during a school year. Explain what the variables and numbers mean.

   b. Use the equation to find the number of correct answers Gilberto needs to buy a new shirt that costs $25. Show your work.

   c. Gilberto answered all 12 problems correctly on his first math exam. How much money is he assured of receiving for the year? Show your work.

11. For parts (a) and (b), find the mystery number and explain your reasoning.

   a. If you add 15 to 3 times the mystery number, you get 78. What is the mystery number?

   b. If you subtract 27 from 5 times the mystery number, you get 83. What is the mystery number?

   c. Make up clues for a riddle whose mystery number is 9.

12. Use properties of equality and numbers to solve each equation for x. Check your answers.

   a. $7 + 3x = 5x + 13$ b. $3x - 7 = 5x + 13$

   c. $7 - 3x = 5x + 13$ d. $3x + 7 = 5x - 13$

13. **Multiple Choice** Which of the following is a solution to the equation $11 = -3x - 10$?

   A. 1.3   B. $-\frac{1}{3}$ C. -7 D. 24

14. Solve each equation for x. Check your answers.

   a. $3x + 5 = 20$ b. $3x - 5 = 20$ c. $3x + 5 = -20$

   d. $-3x + 5 = 20$ e. $-3x - 5 = -20$

15. Determine whether each expression is *always, sometimes,* or *never* equal to $-2(x - 3)$.

   a. $-2x + 6$ b. $-2x - 6$ c. $2x + 6$

   d. $-2x - 3$ e. $-2(x + 3)$ f. $2(3 - x)$

16. For each equation in Group 1, find a matching equation in Group 2 that has the same solution. Write down any strategies you used.

Group 1

A: $3x + 6 = 12$

B: $3x - 6 = 12$

C: $-3x + 6 = 12$

D: $3x + 6 = -12$

E: $6x - 3 = 12$

Group 2

F: $x = 6$

G: $3(2 - x) = 12$

H: $3x = 6$

J: $x - \frac{1}{2} = 2$

K: $x + 2 = -4$

17. Solve each equation. Check your answers.

a. $3(x + 2) = 12$

b. $3(x + 2) = x - 18$

c. $3(x + 2) = 2x$

d. $3(x + 2) = -15$

18. Solve each equation for x.

a. $5 - 2(x - 1) = 12$

b. $5 + 2(x - 1) = 12$

c. $5 - 2(x + 2) = 12$

d. $5 - 2x + 2 = 12$

19. Solve each equation for x.

a. $2x + 6 = 6x + 2$

b. $2x + 6 = 6x - 2$

c. $2x - 6 = -6x + 2$

d. $-2x - 6 = -6x - 2$

For Exercises 20 and 21, use the equation $y = 4 - 3x$.

20. Find y when:

a. $x = 4$ **b.** $x = -3$ **c.** $x = 2$

d. $x = -\frac{4}{3}$ **e.** $x = 0$

21. Find x when:

a. $y = 0$ **b.** $y = 21$ **c.** $y = -15$ **d.** $y = 3.5$

22. Explain how the information you found for Exercises 20 and 21 relates to locating points on a line representing $y = 4 - 3x$.

23. In each part below, identify the equations that have the same solution.

a. A: $x = 8$

B: $-x = 8$

C: $x + 3x = 8$

D: $1x = 8$

E: $8 = 4x$

F: $8 = -1x$

b. G: $x - 1 = 6$

H: $x - 1 = -6$

J: $-x + 1 = -6$

K: $-x + 1 = 6$

L: $6 = 1 - x$

M: $-1 + x = 6$

c. N: $x - \frac{1}{2} = 4$

O: $\frac{1}{2}x = -4$

P: $x = 4 + \frac{1}{2}$

Q: $-\frac{1}{2}x = 4$

R: $\frac{1}{2} - x = 4$

S: $-x + \frac{1}{2} = 4$

24. Two students' solutions to the equation $6(x + 4) = 3x - 2$ are shown below. Both students made an error. Find the errors and give a correct solution.

Student 1

$6(x + 4) = 3x - 2$

$x + 4 = 3x - 2 - 6$

$x + 4 = 3x - 8$

$x + 4 + 8 = 3x - 8 + 8$

$x + 12 = 3x$

$12 = 2x$

$x = 6$ ✗

Student 2

$6(x + 4) = 3x - 2$

$6x + 4 = 3x - 2$

$3x + 4 = -2$

$3x + 4 - 4 = -2 - 4$

$3x = -6$

$x = -2$ ✗

25. Two students' solutions to the equation $58.5 = 3.5x - 6$ are shown below. Both students made an error. Find the errors and give a correct solution.

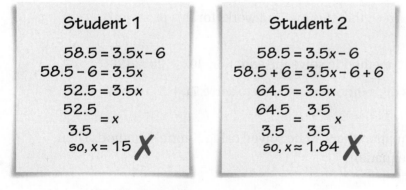

Student 1

$58.5 = 3.5x - 6$

$58.5 - 6 = 3.5x$

$52.5 = 3.5x$

$\dfrac{52.5}{3.5} = x$

so, $x = 15$ ✗

Student 2

$58.5 = 3.5x - 6$

$58.5 + 6 = 3.5x - 6 + 6$

$64.5 = 3.5x$

$\dfrac{64.5}{3.5} = \dfrac{3.5}{3.5}x$

so, $x \approx 1.84$ ✗

26. Describe how you could use a graph or a table to solve each equation.

 a. $5x + 10 = -20$

 b. $4x - 9 = -7x + 13$

27. Use the equation $P = 10 - 2.5c$.

 a. Find P when $c = 3.2$.

 b. Find c when $P = 85$.

 c. Describe how you can use a table or a graph to answer parts (a) and (b).

28. Use the equation $m = 15.75 + 3.2d$.

 a. Find m when:

  i. $d = 20$ **ii.** $d = 0$ **iii.** $d = 3.2$

 b. Find d when:

  i. $m = 54.15$ **ii.** $m = 0$ **iii.** $m = 100$

29. Khong thinks he has a different way to solve equations, by first factoring out both sides of the equation by the greatest common factor. This is how he solved the first equation in Problem 3.4.

> $5x + 10 = 20$ is the same as $5(x + 2) = 5(4)$.
> So, If I divide both sides by 5, I get $x + 2 = 4$.
> This means that $x = 2$.

 a. Is Khong correct, that this method works for this problem? Explain.

 b. Use Khong's method to solve the equation $40x + 20 = 120$.

 c. Khong says his method won't work to solve $7x + 3 = 31$. Why is that?

 d. Write an equation that can be solved using Khong's method. Then solve your equation.

30. The expenses E and income I for making and selling T-shirts with a school logo are given by the equations $E = 535 + 4.50n$ and $I = 12n$, where n is the number of T-shirts.

   a. How many T-shirts must be made and sold to break even? Explain.

   b. Suppose only 50 shirts are sold. Is there a profit or a loss? Explain.

   c. Suppose the income is $1,200. Is there a profit or a loss? Explain.

   d. i. For each equation, find the coordinates of a point that lies on the graph of the equation.

   ii. What information does this point give you?

   iii. Describe how to use the equation to show that the point lies on the graph.

31. The International Links long-distance phone company charges no monthly fee but charges 18 cents per minute for long-distance calls. The World Connections' long-distance company charges $50 per month plus 10 cents per minute for long-distance calls. Compare the World Connections long-distance plan to that of International Links.

   a. Under what circumstances is it cheaper to use International Links? Explain your reasoning.

   b. Write an inequality that describes when each company is cheaper. Represent the solution to the inequality on a graph.

32. Two cell-phone providers have different charges per month for text-messaging plans. Driftless Region Telephone has a plan charging $1\frac{1}{2}$ cents per text, with a monthly rate of $10. Walby Communications charges $16 per month for unlimited texting.

   a. If you were paying for a plan, which one would you purchase? Explain.

   b. Would you make the same recommendation for anyone else?

   c. Write an inequality that would help someone decide which plan to purchase. Then, represent the solution on a graph.

33. Students at Hammond Middle School are raising money for the end-of-year school party. They decide to sell roses for Valentine's Day. The students can buy the roses for 50 cents each from a wholesaler. They also need $60 to buy ribbon and paper to protect the roses as well as materials for advertising the sale. They sell each rose for $1.30.

    a. How many roses must they sell to break even? Explain.

    b. What is the students' profit if they sell 50 roses? 100 roses? 200 roses?

34. Ruth considers buying a cell phone from two different companies. Company A has a cost plan given by the equation $C_A = 32n$, where n is the number of months she has the phone and C_A is the total cost. Company B has a cost plan represented by the equation $C_B = 36 + 26n$, where n is the number of months she is on the plan and C_B is the total cost.

    a. Graph both equations on the same set of axes.

    b. What is the point of intersection of the two graphs? What information does this give you?

Connections

35. Describe what operations are indicated in each expression. Then, write each expression as a single number.

    a. $-8(4)$

    b. $-2 \cdot 4$

    c. $6(-5) - 10$

    d. $2(-2) + 3(5)$

36. Find each quotient.

    a. $\dfrac{12}{-3}$

    b. $\dfrac{-12}{3}$

    c. $\dfrac{-12}{-3}$

    d. $\dfrac{0}{-10}$

    e. $\dfrac{-5}{5}$

    f. $\dfrac{5}{-5}$

    g. $\dfrac{-5}{-5}$

37. Decide whether each pair of quantities is equal. Explain your reasoning.

    a. $6(5) + 2$ and $6(5 + 2)$

    b. $8 - 3x$ and $3x - 8$

    c. $4 + 5$ and $5 + 4$

    d. $-2(3)$ and $3(-2)$

    e. $3 - 5$ and $5 - 3$

    f. 2 quarters and 5 dimes

    g. 1.5 liters and 15 milliliters

    h. 2 out of 5 students prefer wearing sneakers to school and 50% of the students prefer wearing sneakers to school

38. **a.** Use fact families to write a related sentence for $n - (-3) = 30$.
Does this related sentence make it easier to find the value for n?
Why or why not?

    b. Use fact families to write a related sentence for $5 + n = -36$. Does
this related sentence make it easier to find the value for n? Why or
why not?

    c. Solve the equations in parts (a) and (b) using properties of
equality. How does this method compare to using the
fact families?

39. Write two different expressions to represent the area of
each rectangle.

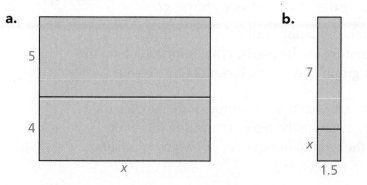

a.

5

4

x

b.

7

x

1.5

40. Find the value of x that makes each equation true.

    a. $3\frac{1}{2}x = \frac{3}{4}$ **b.** $3\frac{1}{2} = \frac{3}{4}x$

    c. $\frac{7}{8}x = \frac{1}{8}$ **d.** $\frac{5}{6} = \frac{3}{4}x$

41. Fill in the missing representation for each inequality.

	In Symbols	On a Number Line	In Words
a.	$x > -4$	(number line with open circle at -4; marks -8, -6, -4, -2, 0, 2)	▪
b.	$x \leq 2$	▪	all numbers less than or equal to 2
c.	$3 < x$	▪	▪
d.	▪	(number line with closed dot at 3; marks -3, 0, 3, 6)	▪
e.	▪	▪	all numbers greater than negative 3

42. The number of times a cricket chirps in a minute is related to the temperature. You can use the formula

$$n = 4t - 160$$

to determine the number of chirps n a cricket makes in a minute when the temperature is t degrees Fahrenheit. If you want to estimate the temperature by counting cricket chirps, you can use the following form of the equation:

$$t = \tfrac{1}{4}n + 40$$

a. At 60°F, how many times does a cricket chirp in a minute?

b. What is the temperature if a cricket chirps 150 times in a minute?

c. At what temperature does a cricket stop chirping?

d. Sketch a graph of the equation with number of chirps on the x-axis and temperature on the y-axis. What information do the y-intercept of the graph and the coefficient of n give you?

43. The higher the altitude, the colder the temperature. The formula $T = t - \frac{d}{150}$ is used to estimate the temperature T at different altitudes, where t is the ground temperature in degrees Celsius and d is the altitude in meters.

a. Suppose the ground temperature is 0 degrees Celsius. What is the temperature at an altitude of 1,500 meters?

b. Suppose the temperature at 300 meters is 26 degrees Celsius. What is the ground temperature?

44. The sum S of the angles of a polygon with n sides is $S = 180(n - 2)$. Find the angle sum of each polygon.

a. triangle   **b.** quadrilateral   **c.** hexagon

d. decagon (10-sided polygon)

e. icosagon (20-sided polygon)

45. Suppose the polygons in Exercise 44 are regular polygons. Find the measure of an interior angle of each polygon.

46. How many sides does a polygon have if its angle sum is

a. 540 degrees?   **b.** 1,080 degrees?

47. The perimeter of each shape is 24 cm. Find the value of x.

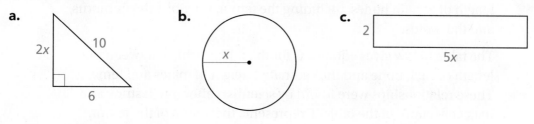

a.   **b.**   **c.**

d. Find the area of the triangle in part (a) and the rectangle in part (c).

48. World Connections long-distance phone company charges $50 per month plus 10 cents per minute for each call.

   a. Write an equation for the total monthly cost C for t minutes of long-distance calls.

   b. Dwayne makes $10\frac{1}{2}$ hours of long-distance calls in a month. How much is his bill for that month?

   c. If Andrea receives a $75 long-distance bill for last month's calls, how many minutes of long-distance calls did she make?

   d. Should the solution to part (c) be written as an equality or inequality? Is it possible that the total number of minutes Andrea was charged was not equal to the amount of time she actually talked on the phone? Explain.

49. As a person ages beyond 30, his or her height can start to decrease by approximately 0.06 centimeter per year.

   a. Write an equation that represents a person's height h after the age of 30. Let t be the number of years beyond 30 and H be the height at age 30.

   b. A 60-year-old female is 160 centimeters tall. About how tall was she at age 30? Explain how you found your answer.

   c. Suppose a basketball player is 6 feet, 6 inches tall on his thirtieth birthday. About how tall will he be at age 80? Explain. (Remember, 1 inch $\approx$ 2.54 centimeters.)

   d. Jena says that in part (a), the equation should actually be written as an inequality. Why might Jena use an inequality to represent this relationship? What inequality do you think Jena has in mind?

50. Forensic scientists can estimate a person's height by measuring the length of certain bones, including the femur, the tibia, the humerus, and the radius.

The table below gives equations for the relationships between the length of each bone and the estimated height of males and females. These relationships were found by scientists after much study and data collection. In the table, F represents the length of the femur, T the length of the tibia, H the length of the humerus, R the length of the radius, and h the person's height. All measurements are in centimeters.

Bone	Male	Female
Femur	$h = 69.089 + 2.238F$	$h = 61.412 + 2.317F$
Tibia	$h = 81.688 + 2.392T$	$h = 72.572 + 2.533T$
Humerus	$h = 73.570 + 2.970H$	$h = 64.977 + 3.144H$
Radius	$h = 80.405 + 3.650R$	$h = 73.502 + 3.876R$

a. About how tall is a female if her femur is 46.2 centimeters long?

b. About how tall is a male if his tibia is 50.1 centimeters long?

c. Suppose a woman is 152 centimeters tall. About how long is her femur? Her tibia? Her humerus? Her radius?

d. Suppose a man is 183 centimeters tall. About how long is his femur? His tibia? His humerus? His radius?

e. Describe generally what the graph would look like for each equation without drawing the specific graph. What do the x- and y-intercepts represent in this problem? Does this make sense? Why?

Humerus

Radius

Femur

Tibia

Extensions

51. The maximum weight allowed in an elevator is 1,500 pounds.

    a. The average weight per adult is 150 pounds, and the average weight per child is 40 pounds. Write an equation for the number of adults A and the number of children C the elevator can hold.

    b. Suppose ten children are in the elevator. How many adults can get in?

    c. Suppose six adults are in the elevator. How many children can get in?

52. Solve each equation. Explain what your answers might mean.

    a. $2(x + 3) = 3x + 3$ **b.** $2(x + 3) = 2x + 6$ **c.** $2(x + 3) = 2x + 3$

53. Frank thinks he can solve inequalities the same way he can solve equations. He uses the method shown below.

> $2x + 6 < 16$
> First, I subtract 6 from both sides. Then I divide by 2.
> This simplifies the inequality to $x < 5$.
>
> My last step is to check my answer.
> $x = 4$ $2(4) + 6 = 14$ $14 < 16$
> $x = 6$ $2(6) + 6 = 18$ $18 \not< 16$

    a. Does Frank's method work in general for other inequalities?

    b. Frank runs into some difficulties trying to solve the following problem:

$$-2x + 1 > 5$$
$$-2x > 4$$

He thinks the answer is $x > -2$. He knows that if this is true, then $x = 0$ should be a solution, because $0 > -2$. But when he checks his work, he notices that $-2(0) + 1 \not> 5$. What numbers should be solutions for the original inequality?

54. Wind can affect the speed of an airplane. Suppose a plane is flying round-trip from New York City to San Francisco. The plane has a cruising speed of 300 miles per hour. The wind is blowing from west to east at 30 miles per hour. When the plane flies into (in the opposite direction of) the wind, its speed decreases by 30 miles per hour. When the plane flies with (in the same direction as) the wind, its speed increases by 30 miles per hour.

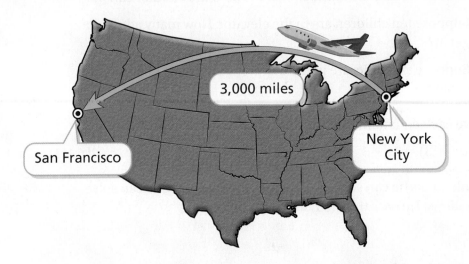

a. Make a table that shows the total time the plane has traveled after each 200-mile interval on its trip from New York City to San Francisco and back.

Airplane Flight Times

Distance (mi)	NYC to SF Time (h)	SF to NYC Time (h)
0	■	■
200	■	■
400	■	■
600	■	■
■	■	■

b. For each direction, write an equation for the distance d traveled in t hours.

c. On the same set of axes, sketch graphs of the time and distance data for travel in each direction.

d. How long does it take a plane to fly 5,000 miles against a 30-mile-per-hour wind? With a 30-mile-per-hour wind? Explain how you found your answers.

55. Students in Mr. Rickman's class are asked to solve the equation $\frac{2}{3}(6x - 9) + \frac{1}{3}(6x - 9) = 3$. Look at the three solutions below. Are they correct? Explain which method makes the most sense to you.

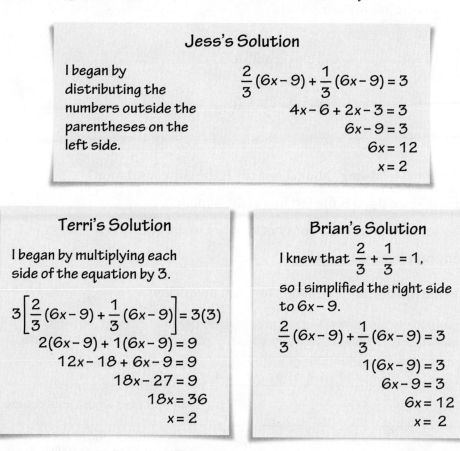

Jess's Solution

I began by distributing the numbers outside the parentheses on the left side.

$$\frac{2}{3}(6x - 9) + \frac{1}{3}(6x - 9) = 3$$
$$4x - 6 + 2x - 3 = 3$$
$$6x - 9 = 3$$
$$6x = 12$$
$$x = 2$$

Terri's Solution

I began by multiplying each side of the equation by 3.

$$3\left[\frac{2}{3}(6x - 9) + \frac{1}{3}(6x - 9)\right] = 3(3)$$
$$2(6x - 9) + 1(6x - 9) = 9$$
$$12x - 18 + 6x - 9 = 9$$
$$18x - 27 = 9$$
$$18x = 36$$
$$x = 2$$

Brian's Solution

I knew that $\frac{2}{3} + \frac{1}{3} = 1$, so I simplified the right side to $6x - 9$.

$$\frac{2}{3}(6x - 9) + \frac{1}{3}(6x - 9) = 3$$
$$1(6x - 9) = 3$$
$$6x - 9 = 3$$
$$6x = 12$$
$$x = 2$$

56. Multiple Choice Dorine solves the equation $3x + 3 = 3x + 9$ and is trying to make sense of her answer.

$$3x + 3 = 3x + 9$$
$$\underline{-3x - 3 \quad -3x - 3}$$
$$0 = 6$$

Which of the following should Dorine say is the correct solution?

A. $x = 6$, because 6 is the final number in the equation.

B. $x = 6$ or $x = 0$, because both of these numbers are in the last equation.

C. There is no solution, because each value of x will lead to $0 = 6$, which is not true.

D. The solution is all numbers, because x will satisfy the equation.

57. Multiple Choice Flora solves an equation similar to Dorine's:

$$3(x + 1) = 3x + 3$$

Flora uses the following method.

$$3(x + 1) = 3x + 3$$
$$3x + 3 = 3x + 3$$
$$\underline{-3x - 3 \quad -3x - 3}$$
$$0 = 0$$

Which of the following should Flora say is the correct solution?

A. $x = 0$, since $0 = 0$ is the last line of the equation.

B. No solution, because x does not show up in the equation $0 = 0$.

C. Any number x will work.

58. Fill in the missing representation for each inequality.

	In Symbols	On a Number Line	In Words
a.	■	(number line from -4 to 4, open circle at 0, arrow right)	all positive numbers
b.	$x^2 < 9$	■	all numbers whose squares are less than 9
c.	■	■	all numbers whose absolute values are greater than or equal to 2
d.	$x^3 > x$	■	all numbers for which the cube of the number is greater than the number itself
e.	$x + \frac{1}{x} > 1$	■	all numbers for which the sum of the number and its reciprocal is greater than 1

59. The Small World long-distance phone company charges 55¢ for the first minute of a long-distance call and 23¢ for each additional minute.

a. Write an equation for the total cost C of an m-minute long-distance call. Explain what your variables and numbers mean.

b. How much does a 10-minute long-distance call cost?

c. Suppose a call costs $4.92. How long does the call last?

Mathematical Reflections 3

In this Investigation, you learned how to solve equations by operating on the symbols. The following questions will help you summarize what you have learned.

Think about these questions. Discuss your ideas with other students and your teacher. Then write a summary of your findings in your notebook.

1. **a.** Suppose that, in an equation with two variables, you know the value of one of the variables. **Describe** a method for finding the value of the other variable using the properties of equality. Give an example to illustrate your method.

   b. Compare the method you described in part (a) to the methods of using a table or a graph to solve linear equations.

2. **a. Explain** how an inequality can be solved by methods similar to those used to solve linear equations.

   b. Describe a method for finding the solution to an inequality using graphs.

3. Give an example of two equivalent expressions that were used in this Investigation. **Explain** why they are equivalent.

Common Core Mathematical Practices

As you worked on the Problems in this Investigation, you used prior knowledge to make sense of them. You also applied Mathematical Practices to solve the Problems. Think back over your work, the ways you thought about the Problems, and how you used Mathematical Practices.

Nick described his thoughts in the following way:

In Problem 3.2, Question A, part (1), we first noted that there are 10 coins on the left and there are 4 coins and 3 bags on the right. So, the three bags must contain a total of 6 coins so that the total number of coins on the right is 10. We figured out that each bag must have 2 coins in it.

But then another group showed us their method. They took four coins off of each side. Now they had 6 coins on the left and 3 bags on the right. They also found that each bag must have 2 coins. Both methods are correct.

Common Core Standards for Mathematical Practice

MP3 Construct viable arguments and critique the reasoning of others.

• What other Mathematical Practices can you identify in Nick's reasoning?

• Describe a Mathematical Practice that you and your classmates used to solve a different Problem in this Investigation.

Exploring Slope: Connecting Rates and Ratios

All of the patterns of change you have explored in this Unit involved constant rates. For example, you worked with walking rates expressed in meters per second and pledge rates expressed in dollars per kilometer. In these situations, you found that the rate affects the following things:

- the steepness of the graph

- the coefficient, m, of x in the equation $y = mx + b$

- how the y-values in the table change for each unit change in the x-values

In this Investigation, you will explore another way to express the constant rate.

Common Core State Standards

7.RP.A.2d Explain what a point (x, y) on the graph of a proportional relationship means in terms of the situation, with special attention to the points $(0, 0)$ and $(1, r)$, where r is the unit rate.

7.EE.A.2 Understand that rewriting an expression in different forms in a problem context can shed light on the problem and how the quantities in it are related.

Also 7.EE.A.1, 7.EE.B.4, 7.EE.B.4a

4.1 Climbing Stairs
Using Rise and Run

Climbing stairs is good exercise, so some athletes run up and down stairs as part of their training. The steepness of stairs determines how difficult they are to climb. By investigating the steepness of stairs, you can find another important way to describe the steepness of a line.

Consider these questions about the stairs you use at home, in your school, and in other buildings.

- How can you describe the steepness of the stairs?
- Is the steepness the same between any two consecutive steps?

Carpenters have developed the guidelines below to ensure that the stairs they build are relatively easy for a person to climb. Steps are measured in inches.

- The ratio of rise to run for each step should be between 0.45 and 0.60.
- The rise plus the run for each step should be between 17 and $17\frac{1}{2}$ inches.

The steepness of stairs is determined by the ratio of the rise to the run for each step. The rise and run are labeled in the diagram below.

Problem 4.1

A 1. Determine the steepness of a set of stairs in your school or home. To calculate the steepness you will need to

- measure the rise and run of at least two steps in the set of stairs.
- make a sketch of the stairs, and label the sketch with the measurements you found.
- find the ratio of rise to run.

2. How do the stairs you measured compare to the carpenters' guidelines on the previous page?

B A set of stairs is being built for the front of the new Arch Middle School. The ratio of rise to run is 3 to 5.

1. Is this ratio within the carpenters' guidelines?

2. Make a sketch of a set of stairs that meet this ratio. Label the lengths of the rise and run of a step.

3. Sketch the graph of a line that passes through the origin and whose y-values change by 3 units for each 5-unit change in the x-values.

4. **a.** Write an equation for the line in part (3).

b. What is the coefficient of x in the equation?

c. How is the coefficient related to the steepness of the line represented by the equation?

d. How is the coefficient related to the steepness of a set of stairs with this ratio?

 Homework starts on page 98.

4.2 Finding the Slope of a Line

The method for finding the steepness of stairs suggests a way to find the steepness of a line. A line drawn from the bottom step of a set of stairs to the top step touches each step at one point. The rise and the run of a step are the vertical and the horizontal changes, respectively, between two points on the line.

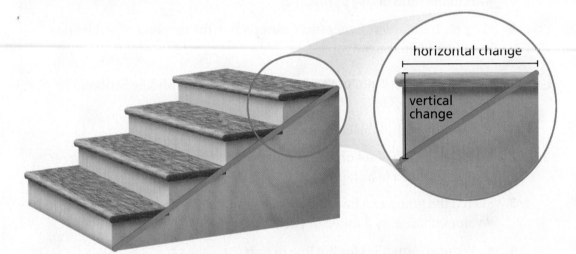

The steepness of the line is the ratio of rise to run, or vertical change to horizontal change, for this step. We call this ratio the **slope** of the line.

$$\text{slope} = \frac{\text{vertical change}}{\text{horizontal change}} = \frac{\text{rise}}{\text{run}}$$

- Does the slope change if we take two stairs at a time?

- Is the slope the same between any two stairs?

Unlike the steepness of stairs, the slope of a line can be negative. To determine the slope of a line, you need to consider the direction, or sign, of the vertical and horizontal changes from one point to another. If vertical change is negative for positive horizontal change, the slope will be negative. Lines that slant *upward* from left to right have *positive slope*. Lines that slant *downward* from left to right have *negative slope*.

The following situations all represent linear relationships.

- For each graph, describe how you can find the slope of the line.

Line With Positive Slope

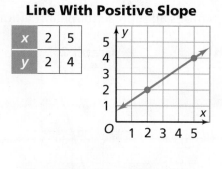

Line With Negative Slope

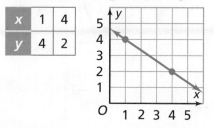

- Describe how you can find the slope of the line that represents the data in the table below.

x	−1	0	1	2	3	4
y	0	3	6	9	12	15

Information about a linear relationship can be given in several different representations, such as a table, a graph, an equation, or a contextual situation. These representations are useful in answering questions about linear situations.

Problem **4.2**

A The graphs, tables, and equations all represent linear relationships.

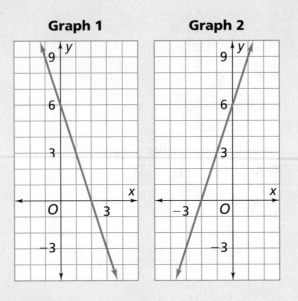

Graph 1   **Graph 2**

Table 1

x	−6	−4	−2	0	2	4
y	−10	−7	−4	−1	2	5

Table 2

x	1	2	3	4	5	6
y	4.5	4.0	3.5	3.0	2.5	2.0

Equation 1

$y = 2.5x + 5$

Equation 2

$y = 20 - 3x$

1. Find the slope and *y*-intercept of the line associated with each of these representations.

2. Write an equation for each graph and table.

Problem 4.2 continued

B The points (3, 5) and (–2, 10) lie on a line.

1. What is the slope of the line?

2. Find two more points that lie on this line. Explain your method.

3. Eun Mi observed that any two points on a line can be used to find the slope. How is Eun Mi's observation related to the idea of "linearity?"

C **1.** John noticed that for lines represented by equations of the form $y = mx$, the points (0, 0) and (1, m) are always on the line. Is he correct? Explain.

2. What is the slope of a horizontal line? A vertical line? Explain your reasoning.

D **1.** Compare your methods for finding the slope of a line from a graph, a table, and an equation.

2. In previous Investigations, you learned that linear relationships have a constant rate of change. As the independent variable changes by a constant amount, the dependent variable also changes by a constant amount. How is the constant rate of change of a linear relationship related to the slope of the line that represents that relationship?

A C E Homework starts on page 98.

4.3 Exploring Patterns With Lines

Your understanding of linear relationships can be used to explore some ideas about groups of lines.

For example, suppose the slope of a line is 3.

- Sketch a line with this slope.

- Can you sketch a different line with this slope? Explain.

In this Problem, you will use slope to explore some patterns among linear relationships.

Problem **4.3**

A Consider the two groups of lines shown below.

Group 1 $y = 3x$ $y = 5 + 3x$ $y = 10 + 3x$ $y = -5 + 3x$

Group 2 $y = -2x$ $y = 4 - 2x$ $y = 8 - 2x$ $y = -4 - 2x$

1. What features do the equations in each group have in common?

2. For each group, graph the equations on the same coordinate axes. What patterns do you observe in the graphs?

3. Describe another group of lines that have the same pattern.

B Consider the three pairs of lines shown below.

Pair 1	**Pair 2**	**Pair 3**
$y = 2x$	$y = 4x$	$y = -3x + 5$
$y = -\frac{1}{2}x$	$y = -0.25x$	$y = \frac{1}{3}x - 1$

1. What features do the equations in each pair have in common?

2. For each pair, graph both equations on the same coordinate axes. What patterns do you observe in the graphs?

3. Describe another pair of lines that have the same pattern.

C Consider the three pairs of lines shown below.

Pair 1	**Pair 2**	**Pair 3**
$y = 2x + 1$	$y = 5 - 2x$	$y = 2(x - 1)$
$y = 2(x + 1) - 1$	$y = 3 - 2(x - 1)$	$y = 4x - 2x - 2$

1. For each pair, graph both equations on the same coordinate axes.

2. What do you notice about the graphs of each pair of equations? How might you have predicted this from the equations?

A C E Homework starts on page 98.

4.4 Pulling It All Together
Writing Equations for Linear Relationships

Throughout this Unit, you have learned several ways to model linear relationships. You have also learned ways to move back and forth between tables, graphs, and equations to solve problems. The next Problem pulls some of these ideas together.

Problem 4.4

A Today is Chantal's birthday. Her grandfather gave her some money as a birthday gift. Chantal plans to put her birthday money in a safe place and add part of her allowance to it each week. Her sister, Chanice, wants to know how much their grandfather gave her and how much of her allowance she is planning to save each week. As usual, Chantal does not answer her sister directly. Instead, she wants her to figure out the answer for herself. She gives her these clues:

> After five weeks, I will have saved a total of $175
>
> After eight weeks, I will have saved $190.

1. How much of her allowance is Chantal planning to save each week?

2. How much birthday money did Chantal's grandfather give her?

3. Write an equation for the total amount of money A Chantal will have saved after n weeks. What information do the y-intercept and coefficient of n represent in this context?

continued on the next page >

Problem 4.4 *continued*

B In the United States, temperature is measured using the Fahrenheit scale. Some countries, such as Canada, use the Celsius temperature scale. In cities near the border of these two countries, weather forecasts present the temperature using both scales.

The relationship between degrees Fahrenheit and degrees Celsius is linear. Two important reference points for this relationship are:

- Water freezes at 0°C, which is 32°F.
- Water boils at 100°C, which is 212°F.

1. Use this information to write an equation relating degrees Fahrenheit and degrees Celsius.

2. How did you find the *y*-intercept? What does the *y*-intercept tell you about this situation?

3. A news Web site uses the image below to display the weather forecast. However, some of the temperatures are missing. Use your equation from part (1) to find the missing temperatures.

Problem 4.4 *continued*

C Square tiles were used to make the pattern below:

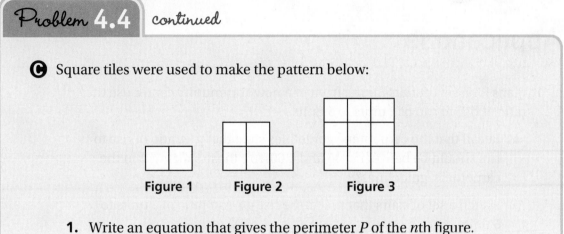

Figure 1   **Figure 2**   **Figure 3**

1. Write an equation that gives the perimeter P of the nth figure.

2. Compare your equation with that of your classmates. Are the expressions for perimeter equivalent? Explain.

3. Is the relationship linear? Explain.

4. Hachi observed that there was an interesting pattern for the number of square tiles needed to build each figure.

    a. What pattern might she have observed?

    b. Write an equation that gives the number of square tiles T in the nth figure.

    c. Is this relationship linear?

D **1.** Look back to the equations you wrote in Question A, part (3); Question B, part (1); and Question C, part (1). Without graphing any of the equations, describe what the graph of each would look like. Which variable would be on the x-axis? Which variable would be on the y-axis? Would the line have a positive slope or a negative slope?

2. When it is helpful to represent a relationship as an equation? A table? A graph?

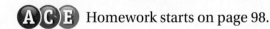 Homework starts on page 98.

Applications

1. Plans for a set of stairs for the front of a new community center use the ratio of rise to run of 2 units to 5 units.

   a. Recall that the carpenters' guidelines state that the ratio of rise to run should be between 0.45 and 0.60. Are these stairs within the carpenters' guidelines?

   b. Sketch a set of stairs that meets the rise-to-run ratio of 2 units to 5 units.

   c. Sketch the graph of a line where the y-values change by 2 units for each 5-unit change in the x-values.

   d. Write an equation for your line in part (c).

2. a. Find the horizontal distance and the vertical distance between the two labeled points on the graph below.

   b. What is the slope of the line?

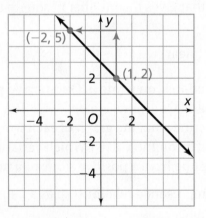

For Exercises 3–6, find the slope and the y-intercept of the line associated with the equation.

3. $y = 10 + 3x$

4. $y = 0.5x$

5. $y = -3x$

6. $y = -5x + 2$

7. Seven possible descriptions of lines are listed below.

    i. positive slope   **ii.** negative slope

   iii. y-intercept equals 0   **iv.** passes through the point $(1, 2)$

    v. slope of zero   **vi.** positive y-intercept

  vii. negative y-intercept

For each equation, list *all* of the descriptions i–vii that describe the graph of that equation.

    a. $y = 2x$ **b.** $y = 3 - 3x$

    c. $y = 2x + 3$ **d.** $y = 5x - 3$

    e. $y = 2$

In Exercises 8–12, the tables represent linear relationships. Give the slope and the y-intercept of the graph of each relationship. Then match each of the following equations with the appropriate table.

        $y = 5 - 2x$ $y = 2x$ $y = -3x - 5$

        $y = 2x - 1$ $y = x + 3.5$

8.

x	0	1	2	3	4
y	0	2	4	6	8

9.

x	0	1	2	3	4
y	3.5	4.5	5.5	6.5	7.5

10.

x	1	2	3	4	5
y	1	3	5	7	9

11.

x	0	1	2	3	4
y	5	3	1	-1	-3

12.

x	2	3	4	5	6
y	-11	-14	-17	-20	-23

13. **a.** Find the slope of the line represented by the equation $y = x - 1$.

  b. Make a table of x- and y-values for the equation $y = x - 1$. How is the slope related to the table entries?

14. **a.** Find the slope of the line represented by the equation $y = -2x + 3$.

  b. Make a table of x- and y-values for the equation $y = -2x + 3$. How is the slope related to the table entries?

15. In parts (a) and (b), the equations represent linear relationships. Use the given information to find the value of b.

  a. The point $(1, 5)$ lies on the line representing $y = b - 3.5x$.

  b. The point $(0, -2)$ lies on the line representing $y = 5x - b$.

  c. What are the y-intercepts in parts (a) and (b)? What are the patterns of change in parts (a) and (b)?

  d. Find the x-intercepts for the linear relationships in parts (a) and (b). (The x-intercept is the point where the graph intersects the x-axis.)

For each pair of points in Exercises 16–19, answer parts (a)–(e).

  a. Plot the points on a coordinate grid and draw a line through them.

  b. Find the slope of the line.

  c. Find the y-intercept of the line. Explain how you found the y-intercept.

  d. Use your answers from parts (b) and (c) to write an equation for the line.

  e. Find one more point that lies on the line.

16. $(0, 0)$ and $(3, 3)$

17. $(-1, 1)$ and $(3, -3)$

18. $(0, -5)$ and $(-2, -3)$

19. $(3, 6)$ and $(5, 6)$

For Exercises 20–22, determine which of the linear relationships A–K fit the description given.

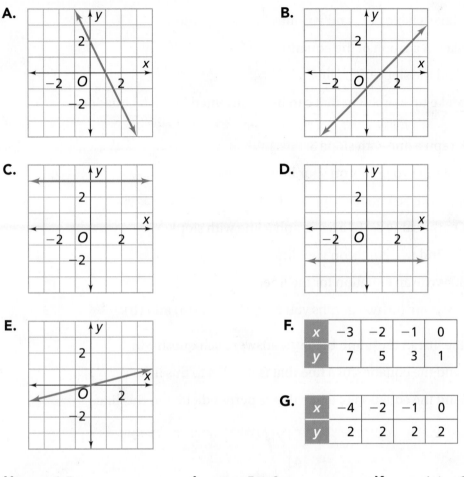

A.

B.

C.

D.

E.

F.

x	−3	−2	−1	0
y	7	5	3	1

G.

x	−4	−2	−1	0
y	2	2	2	2

H. $y = 1.5$ **J.** $y = -5 + 3x$ **K.** $y = 4 + -2x$

20. The line corresponding to this relationship has positive slope.

21. The line corresponding to this relationship has a slope of -2.

22. The line corresponding to this relationship has a slope of 0.

23. Decide which graph from Exercises 20–22 matches each equation.

    a. $y = x - 1$ **b.** $y = -2$ **c.** $y = \frac{1}{4}x$

For each equation in Exercises 24–26, answer parts (a)–(d).

24. $y = x$ **25.** $y = 2x - 2$ **26.** $y = -0.5x + 2$

    a. Make a table of x- and y-values for the equation.

    b. Sketch a graph of the equation.

    c. Find the slope of the line.

    d. Make up a problem that can be represented by each equation.

27. **a.** Graph a line with slope 3.

      i. Find two points on your line.

      ii. Write an equation for the line.

    b. On the same set of axes, graph a line with slope $-\frac{1}{3}$.

      i. Find two points on your line.

      ii. Write an equation for the line.

    c. Compare the two graphs you made in parts (a) and (b).

28. Use the line in the graph below to answer each question.

    a. Find the equation of a line that is parallel to this line.

    b. Find the equation of a line that is perpendicular to this line.

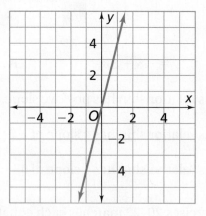

29. a. Find the slope of each line below. Then write an equation for the line.

i.

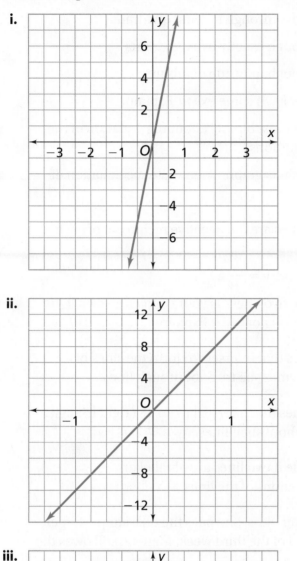

ii.

iii.

b. Compare the slopes of the three lines.

c. How are the three graphs similar? How are they different?

30. Descriptions of three possible lines are listed below.

    i. a line that *does not* pass through the first quadrant

    ii. a line that passes through exactly two quadrants

    iii. a line that passes through only one quadrant

  a. For each, decide whether such a line exists. Explain.

  b. If such a line exists, what must be true about the equation of the line that satisfies the conditions?

  c. If such a line exists, sketch its graph. Then write the equation of the line next to the graph.

31. Suppose the slopes of two lines are the negative reciprocal of each other. For example:

$$y = 2x \text{ and } y = -\frac{1}{2}x$$

What must be true about the two lines? Is your conjecture true if the y-intercept of either equation is not zero? Explain.

32. Write equations for four lines that intersect to form the sides of a parallelogram. Explain what must be true about such lines.

33. Write equations for three lines that intersect to form a right triangle. Explain what must be true about such lines.

34. Describe how you can decide if two lines are parallel or perpendicular from the equations of the lines.

35. Meifeng is taking a bike repair class. She pays the bike shop $15 per week for the class. At the end of the third week, Meifeng still owes the bike shop $75.

  a. How many payments does Meifeng have left?

  b. How much did the class cost?

  c. Write an equation that models the relationship between the time in weeks and the amount of money Meifeng owes.

  d. Without graphing, describe what the graph of this relationship would look like.

36. Robert is installing a patio in his backyard. At 2:00 P.M., he has 120 stones laid in the ground. At 3:30 P.M., he has 180 stones in the ground. His design for the patio says he needs 400 stones total.

   a. When would you predict he will be done?

   b. What is a reasonable estimate for when he started?

   c. If you wanted to know how many stones he would have in the ground at any time, what would be most helpful to you: an equation, a graph, or a table? Explain.

37. At noon, the temperature is 30°F. For the next several hours, the temperature falls by an average of 3°F an hour.

   a. Write an equation for the temperature T, n hours after noon.

   b. What is the y-intercept of the line the equation represents? What does the y-intercept tell you about this situation?

   c. What is the slope of the line the equation represents? What does the slope tell you about this situation?

38. Damon never manages to make his allowance last for a whole week, so he borrows money from his sister. Suppose Damon borrows 50 cents every week.

   a. Write an equation for the amount of money m Damon owes his sister after n weeks.

   b. What is the slope of the graph of the equation from part (a)?

39. In 2000, the small town of Cactusville was destined for obscurity. However, due to hard work by its city officials, it began adding manufacturing jobs at a fast rate. As a result, the city's population grew 239% from 2000 to 2010.

WELCOME TO
CACTUSVILLE
2010 Population
37,000

a. What was the population of Cactusville in 2000?

b. Suppose the same rate of population increase continues. What might the population be in the year 2020?

40. Terrance and Katrina share a veterinary practice. They each make farm visits two days a week. They take cellular phones on these trips to keep in touch with the office. Terrance makes his farm visits on weekdays. His cellular phone rate is $14.95 a month plus $.50 a minute. Katrina makes her visits on Saturday and Sunday and is charged a weekend rate of $34 a month.

a. Write an equation for each billing plan.

b. Is it possible for Terrance's cellular phone bill to be more than Katrina's? Explain how you know this.

c. Suppose Terrance and Katrina made the same number of calls in the month of May. Is it possible for Terrance's and Katrina's phone bills to be for the same amount? If so, how many minutes of phone calls would each person have to make for their bills to be equal?

d. Katrina finds another phone company that offers one rate for both weekday and weekend calls. The billing plan for this company is given by the equation $A = 25 + 0.25m$, where A is the total monthly bill and m is the number of minutes of calls. Compare this billing plan with the other two plans.

41. Three students build the following pattern using the least number of toothpicks possible. For example, Figure 2 uses 5 toothpicks. Suppose that this pattern continues beyond Figure 3.

Figure 1   Figure 2   Figure 3

a. The students are trying to figure out the perimeter of Figure 6 without building it. For each student's method, tell whether you agree or disagree. If you agree, explain why. If you disagree, describe what is incorrect about the student's reasoning.

Juan's Method	Natalie's Method	Steven's Method
From one figure to the next, you are adding one unit of perimeter. Figure 3 has a perimeter of 5 units, so Figure 6 will have a perimeter of 5+1+1+1 = 8 units.	Figure 3 has a perimeter of 5 units. 6 is twice as great as 3. So Figure 6 has twice the perimeter, or 10 units.	Figure 6 will have 6 triangles, and each triangle has a perimeter of 3 units. So Figure 6 will have a perimeter of 6 • 3 = 18 units.

b. The students want to figure out a way to calculate how many toothpicks T they would need to build any figure number F. Which students wrote correct equations? Explain.

Juan's Equation	Natalie's Equation	Steven's Equation
$T = (F + 1) + F$	$T = 2F + 1$	$T = 3F - (F - 1)$
There are $(F + 1)$ slanted toothpicks. There are F toothpicks on the top and bottom.	There are F of this shape in each figure plus one extra toothpick at the end.	There are F triangles, each with 3 toothpicks. But, there are $F - 1$ toothpicks double-counted.

42.

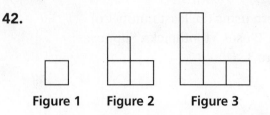

Figure 1   Figure 2   Figure 3

    a. Assume that this pattern continues beyond Figure 3. Write an equation that represents the number of squares S in figure n.

    b. Explain how you know your equation will work for any figure number.

    c. Write two different equations that represent the perimeter P for any given figure number n.

Connections

43. Some hills have signs indicating their steepness, or slope. Here are some examples:

    On a coordinate grid, sketch hills with each of these slopes.

44. Solve each equation and check your answers.

    a. $2x + 3 = 9$ **b.** $\frac{1}{2}x + 3 = 9$

    c. $x + 3 = \frac{9}{2}$ **d.** $x + \frac{1}{2} = 9$

    e. $\frac{x + 3}{2} = 9$

45. Use properties of equality and numbers to solve each equation for x. Check your answers.

    a. $3 + 6x = 4x + 9$ **b.** $6x + 3 = 4x + 9$

    c. $6x - 3 = 4x + 9$ **d.** $3 - 6x = 4x + 9$

46. Use the graph below to answer each question.

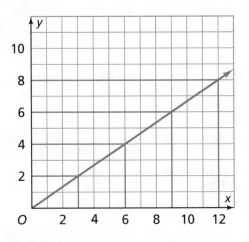

a. Are any of the rectangles in the picture above similar? If so, tell which rectangles, and explain why they are similar.

b. Find the slope of the diagonal line. How is it related to the similar rectangles?

c. Which of these rectangles belong to the set of rectangles in the graph? Explain.

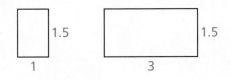

47. The graph below shows the height of a rocket from 10 seconds before liftoff through 7 seconds after liftoff.

a. Describe the relationship between the height of the rocket and time.

b. What is the slope for the part of the graph that is a straight line? What does this slope represent in this situation?

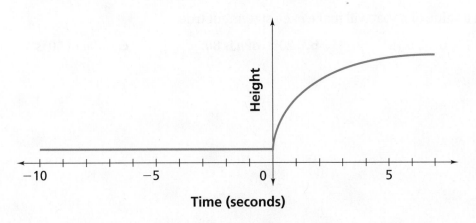

48. Solve each equation. Check your answers.

    a. $2(x + 5) = 18$ **b.** $2(x + 5) = x - 8$

    c. $2(x + 5) = x$ **d.** $2(x + 5) = -15$

49. **Multiple Choice** Which equation has a graph that contains the point $(-2, 7)$?

    A. $y = 4x + 1$ **B.** $y = -x + 5$

    C. $y = 3x - 11$ **D.** $y = -3x + 11$

50. Each pair of figures is similar. Find the lengths of the sides marked x.

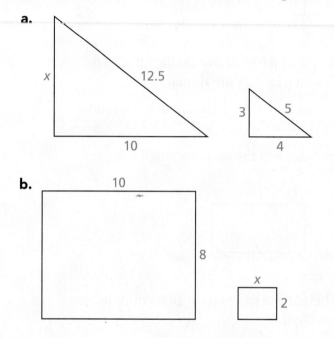

51. Find a value of n that will make each statement true.

    a. $\frac{n}{10} = \frac{3}{2}$ **b.** $\frac{5}{6} = \frac{n}{18}$ **c.** $-\frac{4}{6} = \frac{n}{3}$ **d.** $\frac{5}{18} = \frac{20}{n}$

    e. Write an equation for a line whose slope is $-\frac{4}{6}$.

52. Find a value of n that will make each statement true.

    a. 15% of 90 is n.   **b.** 20% of n is 80.   **c.** n% of 50 is 5.

Extensions

53. On a March flight from Boston to Detroit, a monitor displayed the altitude and the outside air temperature. Two passengers that were on that flight tried to find a formula for temperature t in degrees Fahrenheit at an altitude of a feet above sea level. One passenger said the formula was $t = 46 - 0.003a$, and the other said it was $t = 46 + 0.003a$.

    a. Which formula makes more sense to you? Why?

    b. The Detroit Metropolitan Airport is 620 feet above sea level. Use the formula you chose in part (a) to find the temperature at the airport on that day.

    c. Does the temperature you found in part (b) seem reasonable? Why or why not?

54. Jada's track team decides to convert their running rates from miles per hour to kilometers per hour (1 mile $\approx$ 1.6 kilometers).

    a. Which method would you use to help the team do their converting: graph, table, or equation? Explain why you chose your method.

    b. One of Jada's teammates said that she could write an equation for her spreadsheet program that could convert any team member's running rate from miles per hour to kilometers per hour. Write an equation that each member could use for this conversion.

In this Investigation, you learned that graphs of linear relationships are straight lines. You also learned about the slope, or steepness, of a line. You learned how slope is related to an equation of the line and to a table or a graph of the equation. These questions will help you summarize what you have learned.

Think about these questions. Discuss your ideas with other students and your teacher. Then, write a summary of your findings in your notebook.

1. Explain what the slope of a line is. **How** does finding the slope compare to finding the rate of change between two variables in a linear relationship?

2. **How** can you find the slope of a line from

   a. an equation?

   b. a graph?

   c. a table of values of the line?

   d. the coordinates of two points on the line?

3. For parts (a) and (b), **explain** how you can write an equation of a line from the information. Use examples to illustrate your thinking.

   a. the slope and the y-intercept of the line

   b. two points on the line

Common Core Mathematical Practices

As you worked on the Problems in this Investigation, you used prior knowledge to make sense of them. You also applied Mathematical Practices to solve the Problems. Think back over your work, the ways you thought about the Problems, and how you used Mathematical Practices.

Hector described his thoughts in the following way.

It took our group many steps to solve Problem 4.4, Question A. First, since the amount of money Chantal saved from her weekly allowance is the same each week, we reasoned that the amount of money for each of the weeks between weeks 5 and 8 is a constant.

During this time she saved $190 – $175 or $15. So $15 ÷ 3 weeks is $5 per week. To find the amount of money her grandfather gave her, we found the amount of money she saved from her allowance for the first five weeks, which is 5 × $5 or $25.

Then, we subtracted this amount from $175, and this gave us $150. This is the amount her grandfather gave her for her birthday. We think her grandfather is very generous.

Common Core Standards for Mathematical Practice

MP1 Make sense of problems and persevere in solving them.

- What other Mathematical Practices can you identify in Hector's reasoning?

- Describe a Mathematical Practice that you and your classmates used to solve a different Problem in this Investigation.

Conducting an Experiment

In many situations, patterns become apparent only after sufficient data are collected, organized, and displayed. Your group will be carrying out one of these experiments.

- In Project 1, you will investigate the rate at which a leaking faucet loses water.

- In Project 2, you will investigate how the drop height of a ball is related to its bounce height.

You will examine and use the patterns in the data collected from these experiments to make predictions.

Project 1: Wasted Water Experiment

In this experiment, you will simulate a leaking faucet and collect data about the volume of water lost at 5-second intervals. You will then use the patterns in your results to predict how much water is wasted when a faucet leaks for one month.

Read the directions carefully before you start. Be prepared to explain your findings to the rest of the class.

Materials:

- a watch or clock with a second hand

- a styrofoam or paper cup

- water

- a paper clip

- a clear measuring container (such as a graduated cylinder)

Directions:

Divide the work among the members of your group.

1. Make a table with columns for recording time and the amount of water lost. Fill in the time column with values from 0 seconds to 60 seconds in 5-second intervals (that is, 5, 10, 15, and so on).
2. Use the paper clip to punch a hole in the bottom of the paper cup. Cover the hole with your finger.
3. Fill the cup with water.
4. Hold the paper cup over the measuring container.
5. When you are ready to begin timing, uncover the hole so that the water drips into the measuring container, simulating the leaky faucet.
6. Record the amount of water in the measuring container at 5-second intervals for a minute.

Use this experiment to write an article for your local paper, trying to convince the people in your town to conserve water and fix leaky faucets.

In your article, include the following information:

- a coordinate graph of the data you collected;

- a description of the variables you investigated in this experiment and a description of the relationship between the variables;

- a list showing your predictions for:

  - the amount of water that would be wasted in 15 seconds, 2 minutes, in 2.5 minutes, and in 3 minutes if a faucet dripped at the same rate as your cup does;

  - how long it would take for the container to overflow if a faucet dripped into the measuring container at the same rate as your cup;

  Explain how you made your predictions. Did you use the table, the graph, or some other method? What clues in the data helped you?

- a description of other variables, besides time, that affect the amount of water in the measuring container;

- a description of how much water would be wasted in one month if a faucet leaked at the same rate as your paper cup (explain how you made your predictions);

- the cost of the water wasted by a leaking faucet in one month. (To do this, you will need to find out how much water costs in your area. Then, use this information to figure out the cost of the wasted water.)

Project 2: Ball Bounce Experiment

In this experiment, you will investigate how the height from which a ball is dropped is related to the height it bounces. Read the directions carefully before you start. Be prepared to explain your findings to the rest of the class.

Materials:

- a meter stick
- a ball that bounces

Directions:

Divide the work among the members of your group.

1. Make a table with columns for recording drop height and bounce height.

2. Hold the meter stick perpendicular to a flat surface, such as an uncarpeted floor, a table, or a desk.

3. Choose and record a height on the meter stick as the height from which you will drop the ball. Hold the ball so that either the top of the ball or the bottom of the ball is at this height.

4. Drop the ball and record the height of the first bounce. If the *top* of the ball was at your starting height, look for the height of the *top* of the ball. If the *bottom* of the ball was at your starting height, look for the height of the *bottom* of the ball. (You may have to do this several times before you feel confident you have a good estimate of the bounce height.)

5. Repeat this for several different starting heights.

After you have completed the experiment, write a report that includes the following:

- a coordinate graph of the data you collected;

- a description of the variables you investigated in this experiment and a description of the relationship between the variables;

- a list showing your predictions for:

  - the bounce height for a drop height of 2 meters;

  - the drop height needed for a bounce height of 2 meters;

- a description of how you made your prediction, whether you used a table, a graph, or some other method, and the clues in the data that helped you make your predictions;

- an explanation of the bounce height you would expect for a drop height of 0 centimeters and where you could find this on the graph;

- a description of any other variables besides the drop height, which may affect the bounce height of the ball.

In this Unit, you explored many examples of linear relationships between variables. You learned how to recognize linear patterns in graphs and in tables of numerical data. You also learned how to express those patterns in words and in symbolic equations or formulas. Most importantly, you learned how to interpret tables, graphs, and equations to answer questions about linear relationships.

Use Your Understanding: Algebraic Reasoning

Test your understanding of linear relationships by solving the following problems about the operation of a movie theater.

1. Suppose that a theater charges a school group $4.50 per student to show a special film. Suppose that the theater's operating expenses include $130 for the staff and a film rental fee of $1.25 per student.

   a. What equation relates the number of students x to the theater's income I?

   b. What equation relates the theater's operating expenses E to the number of students x?

   c. Copy and complete the table below.

   Theater Income and Expenses

Number of Students, x	0	10	20	30	40	50	60	70
Income, I ($)	■	■	■	■	■	■	■	■
Expenses, E ($)	■	■	■	■	■	■	■	■

   d. On the same set of axes, graph the theater's income and operating expenses for any number of students from 0 to 100.

   e. Describe the patterns by which income and operating expenses increase as the number of students in a group increases.

   f. Write and solve an equation that you can use to answer the question "How many students need to attend the movie so that the theater's income will equal its operating expenses?"

   g. Write an equation that represents the theater's profit. Compare your equation to those your classmates wrote.

h. Find the number of students that make each of the following inequality statements true.

   i. $E < 255$

  ii. $I > 675$

2. At another theater, the income and expenses combine to give the equation $y = 3x - 115$. This equation relates operating profit and the number of students in a group.

  a. What do the numbers 3 and -115 tell you about:

    i. the relationship between the number of students and the theater's profit?

   ii. the pattern of entries that would appear in a table of sample (*students, profit*) data?

   iii. a graph of the relationship between the number of students and the profit?

  b. Write and solve equations to find the number of students needed for the theater to:

    i. break even (make a profit of $0).

   ii. make a profit of $100.

  c. Write and solve an equation you can use to find the number of students for which the theaters in Exercise 1 and Exercise 2 make the same profit. Then find the amount of that profit.

Explain Your Reasoning

When you use mathematical calculations to solve a problem or make a decision, it is important to be able to justify each step in your reasoning. For Exercises 1 and 2:

3. Consider the variables and relationships.

   a. What are the variables?

   b. Which pairs of variables are related to each other?

   c. In each pair of related variables, how does a change in the value of one variable cause a change in the value of the other variable?

4. Which relationships are linear and which are not linear? What patterns in the tables, graphs, and equations support your conclusions?

5. For a linear relationship, what information do the slope and *y*-intercept of the graph indicate about the relationship?

6. For a linear relationship, how do the slope and *y*-intercept relate to data patterns in the table?

7. Consider the strategies for solving linear equations such as those in Problem 1, part (f) and Problem 2, part (c).

   a. How can you solve the equations using tables of values?

   b. How can you solve the equations using graphs?

   c. How can you solve the equations using symbolic reasoning alone?

8. Suppose you were asked to write a report describing the relationships among the number of students in the group, the theater's income, and the theater's operating expenses. What value might be gained by including the table? Including the graph? Including the equation? What are the limitations of each representation?

C **coefficient** A number that is multiplied by a variable in an equation or expression. In a linear equation of the form $y = mx + b$, the number m is the coefficient of x as well as the slope of the line. For example, in the equation $y = 3x + 5$, the coefficient of x is 3. This is also the slope of the line.

coeficiente Un número que se multiplica por una variable en una ecuación o expresión. En una ecuación lineal de la forma $y = mx + b$, el número m es el coeficiente de x así como la pendiente de la recta. Por ejemplo, en la ecuación $y = 3x + 5$, el coeficiente de x es 3. También representa la pendiente de la recta.

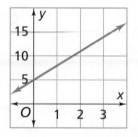

constant term A number in an equation that is not multiplied by a variable, or an amount added to or subtracted from the terms involving variables. In an equation of the form $y = mx + b$, the y-intercept, b, is a constant term. The effect of the constant term on a graph is to raise or lower the graph. The constant term in the equation $y = 3x + 5$ is 5. The graph of $y = 3x$ is raised vertically 5 units to give the graph of $y = 3x + 5$.

término constante Un número en una ecuación que no está multiplicado por una variable o una cantidad sumada o restada a los términos que contienen variables. En una ecuación de la forma $y = mx + b$, el intercepto en y, b, es un término constante. El efecto del término constante hace que una gráfica suba o baje. El término constante en la ecuación $y = 3x + 5$ es 5. Para obtener la gráfica de $y = 3x + 5$, la gráfica $y = 3x$ se sube 5 unidades sobre el eje vertical.

coordinates An ordered pair of numbers used to locate a point on a coordinate grid. The first number in a coordinate pair is the value for the *x*-coordinate, and the second number is the value for the *y*-coordinate. A coordinate pair for the graph shown below is (0, 60).

coordenadas Un par ordenado de números que se usa para ubicar un punto en una gráfica de coordenadas. El primer número del par de coordenadas es el valor de la coordenada *x* y el segundo número es el valor de la coordenada *y*. Un par de coordenadas para la gráfica que se muestra es (0, 60).

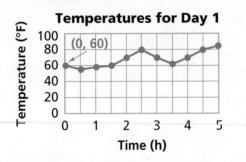

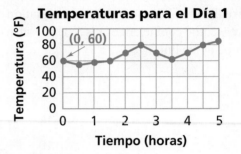

- -

D

dependent variable One of the two variables in a relationship. Its value depends upon or is determined by the other variable called the *independent variable*. For example, the distance you travel on a car trip (dependent variable) depends on how long you drive (independent variable).

variable dependiente Una de las dos variables de una relación. Su valor depende o está determinado por el valor de la otra variable, llamada *variable independiente*. Por ejemplo, la distancia que recorres durante un viaje en carro (variable dependiente) depende de cuánto conduces (variable independiente).

describe Academic Vocabulary
To explain or tell in detail. A written description can contain facts and other information needed to communicate your answer. A diagram or a graph may also be included.

related terms *express, explain, illustrate*

sample Describe how to solve the equation $3x + 14 = 23$.

I can sketch a graph of the line $y = 3x + 14$. When y is 23, the value of x is 3.

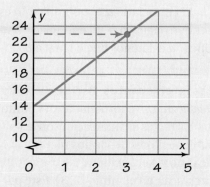

I can also solve for x in the equation $3x + 14 = 23$ by subtracting 14 from both sides to get $3x = 9$. Then I can divide both sides by 3 to get $x = 3$.

describir Vocabulario académico
Explicar o decir con detalle. Una descripción escrita puede contener datos y otra información necesaria para comunicar tu respuesta. También se puede incluir un diagrama o una gráfica.

términos relacionados *expresar, explicar, illustrar*

ejemplo Describe cómo se resuelve la ecuación $3x + 14 = 23$.

Puedo bosquejar una gráfica de la recta $y = 3x + 14$. Cuando y es 23, el valor de x es 3.

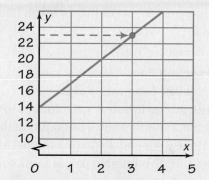

También puedo resolver x en la ecuación $3x + 14 = 23$ restando 14 de cada lado para obtener $3x = 9$. Luego puedo dividir ambos lados por 3 para obtener $x = 3$.

E

equivalent expressions Expressions that represent the same quantity. For example, $2 + 5$, $3 + 4$, and 7 are equivalent expressions. You can apply the Distributive Property to $2(x + 3)$ to write the equivalent expression $2x + 6$. You can apply the Commutative Property to $2x + 6$ to write the equivalent expression $6 + 2x$.

expresiones equivalentes Expresiones que representan la misma cantidad. Por ejemplo, $2 + 5$, $3 + 4$ y 7 son expresiones equivalentes. Puedes aplicar la propiedad distributiva a $2(x + 3)$ para escribir la expresión equivalente $2x + 6$. Puedes aplicar la propiedad conmutativa a $2x + 6$ para escribir la expresión equivalente $6 + 2x$.

independent variable One of the two variables in a relationship. Its value determines the value of the other variable called the *dependent variable*. If you organize a bike tour, for example, the number of people who register to go (independent variable) determines the cost for renting bikes (dependent variable).

variable independiente Una de las dos variables en una relación. Su valor determina el de la otra variable, llamada *variable dependiente*. Por ejemplo, si organizas un recorrido en bicicleta, el número de personas inscritas (variable independiente) determina el costo del alquiler de las bicicletas (variable dependiente).

inequality A statement that two quantities are not equal. The symbols $>$, $<$, $\geq$, and $\leq$ are used to express inequalities. For example, if a and b are two quantities, then "a is greater than b" is written as $a > b$, and "a is less than b" is written as $a < b$. The statement $a \geq b$ means "a is greater than or equal to b." The statement $a \leq b$ means that "a is less than or equal to b."

desigualdad Enunciado que indica que dos cantidades no son iguales. Los símbolos $>$, $<$, $\geq$ y $\leq$ se usan para expresar desigualdades. Por ejemplo, si a y b son dos cantidades, entonces "a es mayor que b" se escribe como $a > b$ y "a es menor que b" se escribe como $a < b$. El enunciado $a \geq b$ significa "a es mayor que o igual a b". El enunciado $a \leq b$ significa "a es menor que o igual a b".

intersecting lines Lines that cross or *intersect*. The coordinates of the point where the lines intersect are solutions to the equations for both lines. The graphs of the equations $y = x$ and $y = 2x - 3$ intersect at the point (3, 3). This number pair is a solution to each equation.

rectas intersecantes Rectas que se cruzan o *intersecan*. Las coordenadas del punto en el que las rectas se intersecan son la solución de las ecuaciones de las dos rectas. Las gráficas de las ecuaciones $y = x$ e $y = 2x - 3$ se intersecan en el punto (3, 3). Este par de números es la solución de las dos ecuaciones.

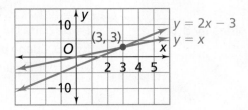

linear relationship A relationship in which there is a constant rate of change between two variables. A linear relationship can be represented by a straight-line graph and by an equation of the form $y = mx + b$. In the equation, m is the slope of the line, and b is the y-intercept.

relación lineal Una relación en la que hay una tasa de variación constante entre dos variables. Una relación lineal se puede representar con una gráfica de línea recta y con una ecuación de la forma $y = mx + b$. En la ecuación, m es la pendiente de la recta y b es el intercepto en y.

origin The point where the x- and y-axes intersect on a coordinate graph. With coordinates $(0, 0)$, the origin is the center of the coordinate plane.

origen El punto en que los ejes de las x y las y se intersecan en una gráfica de coordenadas. Si las coordenadas son $(0, 0)$, el origen es el centro del plano de coordenadas.

point of intersection The point where two lines intersect. If the lines are represented on a coordinate grid, the coordinates for the point of intersection can be read from the graph.

punto de intersección El punto en el que dos rectas se intersecan. Si las rectas están representadas en una gráfica de coordenadas, las coordenadas del punto de intersección se pueden leer en la gráfica.

properties of equality For all real numbers a, b, and c:

Addition: If $a = b$, then $a + c = b + c$.

Subtraction: If $a = b$, then $a - c = b - c$.

Multiplication: If $a = b$, then $a \cdot c = b \cdot c$.

Division: If $a = b$ and $c \neq 0$, then $\frac{a}{c} = \frac{b}{c}$.

propiedades de la igualdad Para todos los números reales a, b y c:

Suma: Si $a = b$, entonces $a + c = b + c$.

Resta: Si $a = b$, entonces $a - c = b - c$.

Multiplicación: Si $a = b$, entonces $a \cdot c = b \cdot c$.

División: Si $a = b$ y $c \neq 0$, entonces $\frac{a}{c} = \frac{b}{c}$.

relate Academic Vocabulary
To have a connection to or impact on something else.

related terms *connect, correlate*

sample Hannah raises $12 for every 3 pies she sells. Write an equation that shows how the total number of pies p she sells relates to the amount of money she raises r.

relacionar Vocabulario académico
Tener una conexión o un impacto en algo.

términos relacionados *unir, correlacionar*

ejemplo Hannah recauda $12 por cada 3 pasteles que vende. Escribe una ecuación que muestre cómo se relaciona el número total de pasteles p que vende con la cantidad que recauda r.

If she raises $12 for selling 3 pies, she raises $4 for every pie, because $\frac{\$12}{4} = 3$. The equation $r = 4p$ shows the relationship.

Si recauda $12 por vender 3 pasteles, recauda $4 por cada pastel, porque $\frac{\$12}{4} = 3$. La ecuación $r = 4p$ muestra la relación.

represent Academic Vocabulary
To stand for or take the place of something else. For example, an equation can represent a given situation, and a graph can represent an equation.

related terms *symbolize, correspond to*

sample A company charges $15 per sweatshirt plus a total shipping fee of $10. Does this represent a linear relationship?

This represents a linear relationship because there is a constant rate of change between the number of sweatshirts and the amount the company will charge.

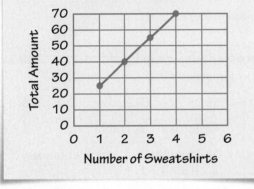

representar Vocabulario académico
Significar o tomar el lugar de algo más. Por ejemplo, una ecuación puede representar una situación dada y una gráfica puede representar una ecuación.

términos relacionados *simbolizar, corresponder*

ejemplo Una compañía cobra $15 por sudadera más una tarifa de envío de $10. ¿Representa esto una relación lineal?

Esto representa una relación lineal porque hay una tasa de cambio constante entre el número de sudaderas y la cantidad que la compañía cobra.

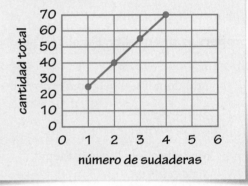

rise The vertical change between two points on a graph. The slope of a line is the rise divided by the run.

distancia vertical La variación vertical entre dos puntos de una gráfica. La pendiente de una recta es la distancia vertical dividida por la distancia horizontal.

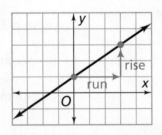

run The horizontal change between two points on a graph. The slope of a line is the rise divided by the run.

distancia horizontal La variación horizontal entre dos puntos de una gráfica. La pendiente de una recta es la distancia vertical dividida por la distancia horizontal.

scale The distance between two consecutive tick marks on the *x*- and *y*-axes of a coordinate grid. When graphing, an appropriate scale must be selected so that the resulting graph will be clearly shown. For example, when graphing the equation $y = 60x$, a scale of 1 for the *x*-axis and a scale of 15 or 30 for the *y*-axis would be reasonable.

escala La distancia entre dos marcas consecutivas en los ejes *x* y *y* de una gráfica de coordenadas. Cuando se hace una gráfica, se debe seleccionar una escala apropiada de manera que represente con claridad la gráfica resultante. Por ejemplo, cuando se grafica la ecuación $y = 60x$, una escala razonable sería 1 para el eje de las *x* y una escala de 15 ó 30 para el eje de las *y*.

slope The number that expresses the steepness of a line. The slope is the ratio of the vertical change to the horizontal change between any two points on the line. Sometimes this ratio is referred to as *the rise over the run*. The slope of a horizontal line is 0. Slopes are positive if the *y*-values increase from left to right on a coordinate grid and negative if the *y*-values decrease from left to right. The slope of a vertical line is undefined. The slope of a line is the same as the constant rate of change between the two variables. For example, the points (0, 0) and (3, 6) lie on the graph of $y = 2x$. Between these points, the vertical change is 6 and the horizontal change is 3, so the slope is $\frac{6}{3} = 2$, which is the coefficient of *x* in the equation.

pendiente El número que expresa la inclinación de una recta. La pendiente es la razón entre la variación vertical y la horizontal entre dos puntos cualesquiera de la recta. A veces, a esta razón se la llama *distancia vertical sobre distancia horizontal*. La pendiente de una recta horizontal es 0. Las pendientes son positivas si los valores de *y* aumentan de izquierda a derecha en una gráfica de coordenadas y negativas si los valores de *y* disminuyen de izquierda a derecha. La pendiente de una recta vertical es indefinida. La pendiente de una recta es igual a la tasa de variación constante entre las dos variables. Por ejemplo, los puntos (0, 0) y (3, 6) están representados en la gráfica de $y = 2x$. Entre estos puntos, la variación vertical es 6 y la variación horizontal es 3, de manera que la pendiente es $\frac{6}{3} = 2$, que es el coeficiente de *x* en la ecuación.

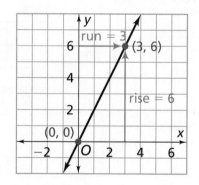

solution of an equation The value or values that make an equation true.

solución de una ecuación El valor o valores que hacen que una ecuación sea verdadera.

solve Academic Vocabulary
To determine the value or values that make a given statement true. Several methods and strategies can be used to solve a problem including estimating, isolating the variable, drawing a graph, or using a table of values.

related terms *calculate, solution*

sample Solve the equation
$4(x - 3) = 2x$.

resolver Vocabulario académico
Determinar el valor o valores que hacen verdadero un enunciado. Se pueden usar varios métodos o estrategias para resolver un problema, entre ellos la estimación, aislar la variable, hacer una gráfica o usar una tabla de valores.

términos relacionados *calcular, solución*

ejemplo Resuelve la ecuación
$4(x - 3) = 2x$.

I can solve the equation by isolating x on the left side of the equation.

$4(x - 3) = 2x$
$4x - 12 = 2x$
$2x - 12 = 0$
$2x = 12$
$x = 6$

I can also solve for x by using a table.

x	4(x – 3)	2x
0	-12	0
3	0	6
5	8	10
6	12	12

The answer is x = 6.

Puedo resolver la ecuación despejando x en el lado izquierdo de la ecuación.

$4(x - 3) = 2x$
$4x - 12 = 2x$
$2x - 12 = 0$
$2x = 12$
$x = 6$

También puedo resolver x usando una tabla.

x	4(x – 3)	2x
0	– 12	0
3	0	6
5	8	10
6	12	12

La respuesta es x = 6.

X **x-intercept** The point where a graph crosses the *x*-axis. In the graph, the *x*-intercept is $(-4, 0)$ or -4.

intercepto en x El punto en el que la gráfica atraviesa el eje de las *x*. En la gráfica, el intercepto en *x* es $(-4, 0)$ ó -4.

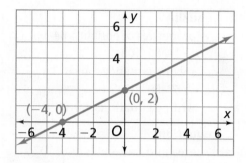

Y **y-intercept** The point where the graph crosses the *y*-axis. In a linear equation of the form $y = mx + b$, the *y*-intercept is the constant, *b*. In the graph, the *y*-intercept is $(0, 2)$ or 2.

intercepto en y El punto en el que la gráfica atraviesa el eje de las *y*. En una ecuación lineal de la forma $y = mx + b$, el intercepto en *y* es la constante, *b*. En la gráfica, el intercepto en *y* es $(0, 2)$ ó 2.

Index

Index

Acknowledgments

Cover Design

Three Communication Design, Chicago

Text

Grateful acknowledgment is made to the following for copyrighted material:

080 National Council of Teachers of Mathematics

From *"Mathematics in Forensic Science: Male and Female Bone Measurements"* by George Knill from MATHEMATICS TEACHER, FEBRUARY 1981.

Photographs

Photo locators denoted as follows: Top (T), Center (C), Bottom (B), Left (L), Right (R), Background (Bkgd)

002 Christina Richards/Shutterstock; **003** Westend61/Westend61/Corbis; **032** Michael Steele/Staff/Getty Images; **087** Dudarev Mikhail/Shutterstock; **088** Les and Dave Jacobs/cultura/Corbis; **105** Christina Richards/Shutterstock; **108** (L) Powered by Light/Alan Spencer/Alamy, (R) Taweesak Jarearnsin/Shutterstock.